RANCHES, RECIPES AND
TALES OF A MISSPENT YOUTH

D1737243

AUTHOR

JIM W. BARRIE

ILLUSTRATOR

KATHY MCCARTHY

****

EDITOR

MOIRE ROBERTSON CREEK

RANCHES, RECIPES AND TALES OF A MISSPENT YOUTH

Copyright © 2021 by **Jim W. Barrie**.

ISBN 9798497611038

Acknowledgements

First and foremost, my wife Stephanie who encouraged me to write these stories and recipes down. Also, Moire Robertson Creek our neighbor who helped with getting it made into a book it wouldn't have happened without you. Also, Tom and Kathy McCarthy it wouldn't have happened without you. Also, Frank and Howard who taught me to start colts and were the best investment of my time in my entire life. Also, all the cowbosses I worked for and the cowboys I worked with those were the greatest times of my life. Also, all the trappers I knew and worked around you guys were the best. Last all the cooks and ranch women that taught me so much about cooking and were part of that life.

Dedication

I dedicate this book to every man who danced to a different drummer and followed a different star and the wives that shared our lives.

Introduction

This book is a collection of stories and recipes from my life and travels on ranches and camps also just plain living alone these times were mostly before Stephanie and I got married; the best thing I ever did they are as I remember them happening but most of them happened a long time ago.

Jim and Stephanie Barrie, 25th Anniversary

How We Got Here

my mothers family on both sides came to California in the beginning of the gold rush the churches settled in nevada county and established buckeye ranch and stage station by the time ww2 came along they had grown the ranch to around eight thousand acres when the war started the government condemned their ranch along with alot of others and mom and her parents came down here to thermalands and bought their ranch mom and my dad got married and then i came along eighteen months later my sister came along we grew up here in thermalands and saw it when it was citrus trees but mostly grade b dairy's later it became a community of people that lived here and worked in town it always was a tight knit community and everyone helped their neighbors we spent the winters and springs here then in the summers we went to the mountains with the cows everyone then lived where there cows did nobody lived down here and ran cattle in the mountains and went just on weekends when we left for the summer we just shut the door to the house and went we didn't even have a key to the house when i was growing up what cars were left here had the keys in them it was a whole different time one of my early memories is of my dad putting me on his horse and leading me around he had a border collie pup and that pup jumped up and bit that horse in the belly and the horse bucked me off and broke both my legs i was in casts up to my hips for six months after that pop was always really upset if he saw anyone letting a small child on a horse i recovered from that and kept on riding and going with pop and grandpa thats how we came here and i got started in the cowboy trade

How the Red Barn Got Here

joe asked how the red barn on mcourtney road got moved down here my family settled in Nevada county during the gold rush and established buckeye ranch and stage station their ranch and many others were condemned for the war effort in world war two the red barn was built around 1900 and when the buckeye was taken grandpa hired a man named Holcomb to move it down here and build it back again so they dismantled it and hauled it down here and set it back up it had a full shearing shed for 10 men and other sheep working facilitys around it after grandpa died pop tore out the shearing shed and built 8 tie stalls and one box stall for horses and the shed on the other side and back were for cows and a place to pull calfs when the war started the people that owned those ranches were promised they could buy them back after they were no longer needed after the war the government backed out on that promise and sold those places at auction almost no one who had owned them before were able to buy them back our family included that also was the beginning of the spenceville wildlife area I asked my mother one time why they didn't drive a harder bargan and she said people were patriotic and it was for the war effort at one time you could call any trucking outfit from Arizona to montana and someone there would know where the red barn north of Lincoln was we used it for a headquarters and everything that got bought landed there and got processed and then hauled out to where ever they were going they also used it to store hay in when we used to go to the mountains pop would call the hay dealer and we would leave the doors open when we got back in the fall that barn would be full of stacked clear to the rafters just a little history of the red barn

Mr Bulloch And The Gypsies

when I was a small boy thermalands was a much smaller community than
it is now but it was just as close knit as it is now everyone watched out for
one another most of the places were small farms and ranches or dairy's a
few people worked out but not very many on our road we had mr
Gordon mr bullock mrs peckham and us we were at the end one fall we
were down here and my dad was in the mountains one evening some
gypsies came to our house and wanted a job painting the buildings mom
told them we didn't hire anyone and they got real aggressive and she
started backing away from them mr bullock had seen the gypsies go by
and was watching with binoculars he came tearing down the road in his
pickup and jumped out with a sixshooter and told those gypsies the get

the hell out of here and never come back the gypsies took off and never did come back just the way neighbors were then

Our First Brush with the Law

I thought I would tell a different story about how we grew up grandpa had several guys working for him over our early years and they were all batchelors and didn't go to town often they were good to my sister and I but when they went to town they always got in trouble with the law and often ended up in jail so we decided early on that the law just waited for someone to come from a ranch and put them in jail so we were scared of anybody we thought was the law including cops game wardens firemen forest service guys anybody that had a badge except the local constable he had got my dad to track a lost guy for him on bear river and rode horses so we thought he was ok even if he was the law between not going to town much and living in cowcamp all summer we were like 2 coyote pups about that time in our lives well we got the idea one day it would be fun to play with matches so we were down at the end of the drive way doing it and started a fire in the grass we tried to stomp it out but couldent so we ran to the house and told my parents some firebug set a fire dad ran out and put it out with a wet sack and mom called the fire dept while this was going on we took cover I went to the barn and hid on top the hay and my sister crawled under the horse trailer of course mom came down to the barn and said if I didn't come down off there she was going to climb up and get me being well acuanted with what happed if she had to climb up there I came down she grabbed me by the arm and we went to the horse trailer where she crawled under and got me sister by the ancle and drug her out from under there by this time im thinking we are probley going to get put in jail or the gas chamber she marches us down to the burned place and there he is the law the biggest meanest looking fireman I had ever seen he made my stand in front of him and put my sister on his knee bear in mind im 5 and shes 4 and told us that they put kids like us in jail sometimes for doing things like starting fires my sister kept turning away from him and he kept making her face him afterwords I asked her what she was doing and said there was a big rock there and if she could have got it she would have hit him in the head with it so we didn't get put in jail luckily she didn't get hold of it after he gave us a big talking to he told us he was letting us go this time if we never played with matches again we sure didn't play with matches after that that's the story of our first brush with the law

Our Dirty Songs

when we were young kids grandpa had several older men working for him they were all batchelors and their language was pretty spectacular they also favored dirty songs since we heard so much of that language mom instead of telling us not to say those things just told us to go right ahead just make sur you get off by your self where no one can hear you and go ahead around our camp in the mountains there was a lot of second growth fir trees we used to get out in those fir trees and just roar out the dirty songs we heard also cuss like it was going out of style I don't know if mom ever heard us or not but no one ever said anything about it

The Bucket Calfs

when I grew up our neighborhood was a lot smaller and more agriculture than it is now the places there were here were ranches or farms and a lot of people had little grade b dairies and milked cows we ran beef cows we always had some calfs we raised on the bottle and we called them the bucket calfs because when they got some age on them you could get them to drink milk out of a bucket and it made feeding them a lot quicker we also just turned them loose everyday around the house to eat grass we lived on the end of the road so they could go up the road and feed the sides of the road they could go about a half a mile every nite we called them and they usually came home but as they got older and the grass got better sometimes they didn't come home so well one after noon I went out to put the bucket calfs away and I called and called and they just looked at me and wouldent come so I went up the road and tried to drive them home bucket calfs don't drive well even if its somewhere they want to go let alone if it isn't there idea so they wernt having any of it by the time I walked home I was mad at them calfs my dad was gone somewhere so I thought ill just send the dogs after them now pops dogs were good ones but they were pretty hardheaded and really rough even tho they were border collies they could stop any kind of cows anywhere and they didn't try and stare something where they wanted it they attacked immediately and kept it up until you stopped them so i untied both of them and told them to get ahead they went around the calfs and proceded to eat them alive about that time mom came out to see how its going just in time to see the calfs come into the yard with both dogs chewing on them she was able to get the dogs stoped and tied up then I got a spanking and she said she was going to tell pop well I think he saw the humor in it because he just told me not to work the dogs anymore but the bucket calfs sure come when you called them after that

Hot Dogs and Eggs

4 potatoes
1 onion
1 bell pepper or can of Chilis
6 eggs
1 package hot dogs

Slice potatoes, dice onion and pepper, cut hotdogs in 2 inch pieces. Cook together till potatoes are about done. Beat eggs. Sometimes I add milk or water. Dump in mixture and cook till done. Cook on low 7 hours. Top with cheese. When cheese melts its done.
Very good with LaVictoria red taco sauce.

***We cooked this in the crock pot.

Buck Steak

One round steak or London broil or chuck roast
flour or Bisquick
eggs (you can or don't have to use them. I don't usually)
cast iron pan
olive oil

Slice meat in strips and dredge in flour or egg and flour.
I also salt and pepper the flour before I start.
Put pan on stove, add about ½ inch of olive oil, turn on heat and wait until oil starts to shimmer when you look across it. Fry meat in bunches. Might have to add oil.

Gravy
Water or milk or canned milk and water and flour. Mix, pour most of the grease out of the pan. Leave 3 tablespoons full and flour and liquid and stir on low till it thickens.

When you go to camp, always take bleach and bleach the dishes once a week. "One capful in the dishwater"

Driving Cows from the Gold Fields

when I was a kid growing up here nobody hauled cows anywhere in fact there were no gooseneck trailers in this part of the country they had racks on the pickups and stock trucks and that was all so if you were going to move cows any where close you drove them one spring my dad and myself I was 5 and my cousin casey he was 12 went over to the yuba vineyard which is right across from the yuba consolidated goldfields on Hammonton-smartsville road and gathered 120 pairs cows and calfs and drove them up the road and around the east side of beale airforce base and to the peckam place which is right next to the shooting range at spenceville we left them there overnite and were back before daylight the next morning and crossed dry creek at the cabbage patch bridge went on across the fish and game and down and crossed rock creek then went down and crossed bear river on the old bridge camp far west lake hadent been built yet then on to the red barn on mcourtney road pretty big trip for a five year old and a twelve year old kid but just part of the life then

My First Horse Wreck

at the age of 5 I thought it was just a matter of time and practice before I would be a cowboy like my dad and everyone else we knew my dad wasent much to rope things for fun he liked to try and keep our cows somewhat gentle but when he got mad he wasent above stiching it on some old bag and jerking her down and letting the dogs chew on her awhile they always got in the bunch and stayed there afterword funny how that always works so well there was an old man from Nevada working on a ranch down the road and he gave me a wore out rope of his so I roped the dogs and the pet lambs and the bottle calfs pretty often so times when pop was watching sometimes when no one was watching my dad had told me not to rope off my pony because I didn't know how to dally and would cut my fingers off however one day I was riding my pony my dad was gone fixing fence and mom was in the house so I decided I was going to rope the bottle calfs since I wasent supposed to dally I just tied my rope to the horn I went I the corrall and roped one of the calfs and of course he ran around behind my pony and rimfired him real good he promply bucked me off and knocked me cold in the mean time my mother heard the commotion and saw the dust and came out to see what was happening by the time she got to the corrall every thing was stopped and the calf choked down and I was comeing to mom got my rope off the calf and caught my pony and made sure I was alright then she picked up an oak stick and gave me a world class spanking needless to say my cowboy career got put on hold for a couple weeks and my rope got hung up in the tack room for a good while

Getting Bucked Off Across the Lake

the last few stories I told were where things always went well this one things didn't go so well when you went cowboying you went for how ever long and what ever happened we were always a long ways from the truck if we had the truck at all some times we rode from home those days we useally moved cows somewhere and a lot of times on the way home we would check other bunches of cows my dad was trying out a new pony for us kids he was as big as a small horse I had rode him around the corrals and around the house and he seemed fine so I was rideing him and he did good moveing the cows and did good checking cows we were on our way back home from the wildlife area when you drive around camp far west lake on the north side theres a set of corrals and a gravel road that goes down into the water before the lake I that road went down and crossed rock creek and went to the bear river bridge we were rideing down that gravel road and for some reason this pony started bucking and bucked me off right on that gravel road we were going down hill so I went right over his right shoulder and lit on my elbows and belly it knocked the wind out of me and skinned me from my wristes to my elbows then the pony took off for home pop had to go catch him and bring him back the dogs stayed with me and I don't mind telling you I bawled and sniveled some but when he got back I had to get back on him and ride him home it was still quite a ways and felt even longer to me needless to say that pony didn't make the cut and got sent back

Driving Cows Out of the Mountains

when I was 6 they still drove the cows out of the mountains so I got to miss 2 weeks of school and go help my dad thought it might be the last year and it was we started at haypress camp and trailed the haypress Lincoln valley and pass creek cows down across where Jackson meadows resevior is now to the big meadow at English dam we stayed at English dam camp they spent a couple days getting ready to go cut out some lame cows ect while we were doing that myself and the crew were up at the big meadow and they were talking there language was spectacular for a six year old boy to listen to I guess they kind of forgot I was there and I didn't do any talking I was learning to much as I sat there on my black pony I thought man I have arrived in this line of work when I can listen to this and not get sent somewhere else the next day we trailed the whole bunch down to hayses corrall and left early the next mourning for Columbia hill which was down by north san juan it took us 2 Or 3 days to get down there but grandpa had rented a field to stay in every night we trailed around bowman lake and thru Graniteville when we got down to Columbia hill there was a one room school house across the road from the field we were going in my dad had came back to the drag and got me and took me to the lead with him and tom so when we came in there I was with the leaders if sure felt important especially because those kids that went to that school were outside watching us the next day they shipped the calfs so my sister and I went over to that school and played with those kids the teacher asked us if we wanted to set in with the class we had a lot of fun doing that and mom was glad because she knew where we were and we wernt in the way the next day they loaded the cows on trucks and sent them to beale and the gold fields we would later go scatter them all over and start calving when I got back to school here the teacher asked me where I had been and I told her she told me I shouldn't tell lies like that when I went home and told mom about it she went right up there and gave that teacher an earful about our life I sure would have liked to hear that conversation but I knew it couldent possibly compare to what I learned up in the big meadow at English dam

Natural Horsemanship

when I was a kid natural horseman ship hadent been invented I personly think the way we do things now is better and sure easier on horses but them old guys could sure make their point with a horse also my dad was always tradeing horses and we had a bob tail truck with a drop ramp on the back those colts didn't want to load up that ramp but he made them fear him worse than the ramp early form of make the wrong thing hard and the right thing easy also horses then were more likely to be tough about there feet well if hes going to be tough to shoe we will just pack salt on him barefoot awhile lets start with 300 pounds and when we get to the salt ground try and pick his feet up he wont let you pick up his feet lets load 300 pounds of rocks on him and haul it back to camp after two or three days of that they all got a better out look on being shod funny thing they all got easy to shoe by the end of summer same thing with one that wanted to buck pack enough salt and rocks on them and they got gentle also early form of making right easy and wrong hard old buck that worked for grandpa had a big old horse he called rawhide that they hauled in the pickup with racks on it he would weave back and forth

12

when they went down the road it made the pickup impossible to steer buck kept and oak limb in the front with him and would reach out the window with it and give old rawhide a few whacks along side of the head still making standing easy and weaveing difficult just a comparison between then and now

Pops Dogs

my dad was an outstanding dog man he always had good dogs I think he just liked training them if one got old or he saw one he thought would suit him better he gave the one he had away and try a new one he liked them hard headed and un controlable he was rough on them and they worshiped the ground he walked on he also expected absolute loyalty out of them there was a guy running cows with us and he was always trying to get pops dog to follow him I asked pop why don't you say something to him his reply was that dog knows who he belongs to and that guy could be feeding him a steak and he would follow me if I called also if he ever followed him off when he came back I would kill him and get one not so un loyle as to follow someone else when I was growing up the border collies were much different I never even saw a dog with eye till I was in high school we would be rideing down some ridge in the mountains and hear bells off in a canyon those bells might start moveing and pop would send the dogs the next thing you heard was timber cracking and bells running back tword you when the dogs got there they attacked imeadatly and kept it up till you stoped them pop also wouldent keep one if they wernt rough and had a lot of bite one of his best ones came from a sheep guy and killed sheep one after another he sure made a great cow dog tho all the ranchers raised pups and traded dogs back and forth also no one worked a dog from in front of the herd they always sent he dogs ahead no fancy directional command either just holler get

13

ahead if he went the wrong way stop him and send him again pretty soon they got so they never went the wrong way

Cowboy Macaroni

3 pounds hamburger
2 onions
3 bell peppers
Minced garlic
3 14½ ounce diced tomatoes
2 8-ounce cans tomato sauce
1 ½ boxes dry pasta or can use 2 boxes

Brown hamburger, add onions, peppers and garlic and tomatoes and tomato sauce
Also add 53 ounces of water. Or, add one of each can you used of water. Bring to a boil and simmer till onions and peppers are done. Add dry pasta. Wait 1 minute and stir it so it don't stick together. Simmer 12 minutes until noodles are done. They will drink the water.

** You can also make this with 6 slices bacon cut up and one package linguisa split in half and sliced.

Hodge Podge

2 cans hominy
2 cans minestrone soup
2 cans tomatoes with chili
2 8 ounce cans tomato sauce
2 cans ranch chili beans (I use ranch beans)
2 onions chipped
minced garlic to taste
2 pounds hamburger browned.

Brown hamburger meat. Add everything and bring to a boil. Simmer 30 minutes, or put in crock pot and cook on low 8 hours.

When your in camp whenever you open a can cut the other end out and flatten it. They take up less room that way and cows don't get them on their feet.

My First Day of School

yesterday our neighbor was by with her son and was telling me about his school work hes a third grader and a great kid and it made me think of my first day of school here is what i thought of my first day of school mom had been pumping me up about going to school and i was all set to go so the big day arrived and i wore my new levies and a green shirt i liked and mom had me stand out on the lawn for a picture in my new clothes with my lunch bucket then she loaded me up in the car and hauled me over to the little country school and went in to talk to the teacher i only knew one kid in the school my friend rickey but he was in forth grade and the first second and third graders had to stay on the other end of the school that morning pretty soon mom left and the teacher rang the bell and i had no idea what that meant so she had to come get me so we didnt get off to a very good start the next thing that happened is we were all talking and she wore this police whistle around her neck and she started blowing that and told us to sit down and be quiet after awile she had us go out on the lawn and pair up with the second and third graders and play some moronic rabbit hop game i thought to myself why dont we play we are loading cows or working in the saleyard or something like that instead of hopping around here like idiots then after that we went back in the class room and tried to write that was a disaster i didnt know anything about that and wasent very coordinated and she kept tooting on her whistle and telling me jim pay attention about halfway thru this i thought to myself they are down at the red barn getting ready to go trail cows out of the mountains so im out of here and got up and walked out and started down the road to the red barn the teacher ran out and called and if i had enough sense i would of took of running but i came back instead and she asked me where i was going i told her i was going to the red barn to help get ready to go back to the mountains she told me i had to go to school now and we didnt just get up and walk out i told her i didnt need to go to school she told me to go sit at my desk and went and talked to the other teacher next came lunch resess me and the other first grade boys were sitting eating our lunches they were cussing so i thought these kids dont know how to cuss so i showed them what i knew about it i was kid of the hour then but the teacher heard me and blew her whistle at me and said jim we dont talk like that on the playground i thought to myself i wish i was bigger i would tell you where you could shove that whistle after that we went back in and tried to count i had never counted and didnt know my numbers at all so that was a disaster also after that we got on the bus and went home and i told mom i was never going back again and she told me if i didnt go back the truant officer would arrest me thats the story of my first day of school

The Rock Target at School

above i told you about my first day of school well i had to keep going but got to go to the mountains and trail cows out of the mountains so when i got back and after the teacher asked me where i had been and i told her and she told me i shouldent tell lies like that i settled in there was a kid in first grade that was a year older than the rest of us and also was a bully he used to line us up and slug us in the belly pretty often we were all kind of scared of him because he was bigger there were 5 boys in first grade one day he lined us up and i dont know how we did it because we didnt plan it ahead of time but we all jumped on him and got him down and worked him over real good he had to stay home for a week and heal up but he left us alone after that the teachers never said anything to us about that either after that incident we got to throwing rocks at one another so the teacher got a sheet of plywood and told two of the third grade boys to paint a boy on that plywood they got to stay outside and do that job while the rest of us were inside she told us if we wanted to throw rocks to throw them at this board with this picture of a boy on it resess finely came and we all went out to see this plywood including the teacher it was standing up against the fence compleat with a junk package drawn on it the teacher turned it around and told us we wouldent be able to use it that day because it wasent finished yet but the next day it was avalible and we all got to throw rocks at it we sure became more accurate rock throwers after that also

Christmas When I Was Little

im setting here thinking about christmas comeing i got to thinking about when i was a kid when we went to the high mountains the cows came home in november and they took the bells off and got them scattered for the winter then layed buck murch off for the winter then you had some shorter days unless you had to start feeding cottonseed we always looked forward to christmas on christmas eve we went down to grandpa churchs for dinner then everybody exchanged gifts this one particular christmas they had lots of presents under the tree and i saw two sheepskin rugs way down on the bottom of the pile i thought i sure would like one of those rugs but a valuble gift like that some adult will probly get i couldent see the nametag on them and you sure didnt touch anything over there finely grampa went over and sat in his chair and started picking up gifts and reading the names on them we all got lots of great things and last i got one of those rugs and my sister got the other one i had mine for years until after stephanie and i got married

Riding Pens on Christmas Day

when i got bigger and we ran cows in sierra valley in august everybody would come home to start getting ready to buy cattle except me i stayed in sierra valley with our cows until about the middle of november pop would come up and we would ship all the calvey cows home so we didnt have any more calfs born up there and i stayed up there with the pairs my job was to ride everyday and make sure there wernt any sick calfs and doctor any that were sick also my dad had a partner that had cows up there and i looked at his cows also he didnt ship his heavy cows home so they were calving all fall also the house i lived in didnt have water or electricity and was a two story house so it got pretty cold along in the fall the water in the bucket would get ice on the top almost every night i would get up and fix breakfast and leave and by the time i got back the house would be cold again build a fire and get warm and leave again when i got back in the afternoon same thing but i didnt mind as i had a good bedroll and was liveing my ambition of being a cowboy about december first we would start shipping pairs home and useally i got home about the fiveteenth but one year it didnt rain untill late and i stayed till the week before christmas that year mom and my sister did my christmas shoping for me and i arrived with my horses and the last of the cows the twenty third of december it sure was nice to get down here where it was warm and you had a shower and hot water that christmas was one of the best we ever had because for once we were caught up on the work and didnt have to feed anything on christmas day or doctor anything i was really looking forward to takeing the whole day off i had a freind that was working at a feedlot close by and he told me he had to ride pens on christmas day by himself and it would take him all day to get done so i offered to go help him and thats how i spent half my day off but we got it done in half the time it was going to take him and we both got a half day off thats where i learned christmas isnt just for you its for everyone and should be shared by everyone

Dogs On Our Bed Tarps

one morning i went with stephanie to feed her goats it was pretty frosty and i told her this story she said i should share it so here it is when we went to the high mountains in the summer we lived at a camp and took care of our cows the camp wasnet very big but it had porches on each side of it my sister and i slept out on the porch all summer and thru the fall if it rained we moved inside and slept on the kitchen floor from the time we were five or six years old we had bedrolls not sleeping bags but bedrolls with a tarp and every thing so sleeping outside wasent any big deal on our range it started getting frosty at night in august and kept it up all fall i can remember lots of mornings wakeing up and haveing frost on our bed tarps the dogs stayed loose at night and would all be curled up on our tarps mabey a smart one might crawl under the tarp with you we always got up at daylight or before and mom would have the stove going and it warm in there you sat up and dressed in bed pulled your boots on and went to the outside sink and washed your face and combed your hair and went in for breakfast by seven oclock we would be saddled up and on our way somewhere at night you could see millions of stars and when we learned about stars in school you could see all the constalations real good every time im down at the barn on a frosty morning and sit on a bale of hay and my dogs get up there with me cause they are cold i think of the mountains and sleeping on the porch

Valley View School

this story is about the school its self my mother went to school there when she was a girl and when i started there it went from first to eigth grade there never were more than fifty kids in all eight grades and they all lived in thermalands you had plenty of one on one with the teachers and personly i would have never made it anywhere else at resess we played baseball or the hill game anything that required a team took at least three grades to make up two teams all the kids knew each other and got along most of the time the older ones helped the smaller ones alot of the time when we had a school play everyones parents came and watched all in all it wasent a bad place to go to school and grow up i never understood why the school district waited until there were more kids out here than ever before to close that school but im proud that its become our community center

Rideing the Grader

when we were growing up for a few years my sister and i were the only kids on our road and we walked a half mile out to the county road to catch the bus when we got off the bus if we were walking home and someone came along they would most always give us a ride home not like today when your scared to even let your kids walk home let alone get in a vehicle with someone we never even thought of things like getting kidnaped sometimes the county road crew were working on our road and they would give you a ride home in the dump truck that was really cool but if you were really lucky jerry or willard would be gradeing all the county dirt roads and you would get a ride home on the grader now that was way cool because we had never even seen many graders up close let alone got a ride home on one it sure was a different time then

The Bird Heads

when I was six I started school at the two room school house up the road while I really looked forward to going to school once I got there after my first day I hated it and continued to hate it all the way thru high school I also didn't get along with the teachers very well they thought I was strange 45 years later I was diagnosed with aspergers syndrome but they didn't even know about aspergers then earler that year I had inherited a bb gun from one of my cousins and after a lot of teaching and practice so I knew how to handle it properly I got turned loose with it every one had wood sideing and most had shingle roofs so everyone hated woodpeckers so I was told to shoot the woodpeckers it took me awhile to get where I could kill them but the first one I got my dad pulled his head off and nailed it on the shop wall I thought that was really cool my first hunting trophy to bad I couldent show it to my friends so one day I had a pretty good hunt and killed 3 woodpeckers I got a board and nailed there heads on it and hid them outside and the next morning I took them to school for show and tell the kids thought it was great and the teacher didn't say much altho she didn't seem impressed with my hunting trophys a few days later a real nice lady showed up at school and talked to me for the better part of three days asked me lots of questions and gave me several test man she was really interested in my hunting I found out years later that she was a phsycoligist I always wanted to see that report I also was told not to bring anymore hunting trophys for show and tell

Health and Hygiene at School

when I was going to school once a year we had health for one week we studied about basic hygiene and one day the health nurse came out and asked the class how often they brushed their teeth and combed there hair ect there were lots of places in our neighbor hood that hauled drinking water and just had ditch water in the house if you were lucky like us you had a spring that you pumped out of ditch water wasent treated and was pretty muddy a lot of times so anyway back to school the first year I went to school the health nurse was there and was asking every body how often they took a bath most of the kids said once a week my mother made us take a bath everynite but I didn't want to look like a sissy in frount of my friends so when she asked me I said I took a bath once a month both her and the teacher said that wasent often enough the next when I got home from school my mother met me at the door and sat me down the health nurse had called her and asked why I only took a bath once a month mom asked me in that very calm tone mothers only use when there puzzeled as to why you said or did whatever before they work you over of course I said I don't know at which point she grabbed me and gave me a world class spanking

What I Learned Instead of School

i imagine some of you are wondering why as much trouble as i had in school why my parents let me stay home and help as much as they did well at home i was learning a trade and how to run cows also things like take care of your horse and dont ride him any harder than you have to you might have to ride him every day all fall also when someone is counting cows string them by in front of him slow and get up behind him and dont let any go behind him this was really important in the mountains because of the timber there went alot of places you could count a big bunch of cows also when you trail cows get them paired up when you start out and let the drag alone so they string out so they stay paired up when you drive them down a paved road very far when your going up a hill get a lead bunch and when you get to the top pass the lead bunch and hold them back going down hill when a cow trots down hill on pavement every time she steps her feet slide if your going very far and let them trot down hill you will have alot of lame cows also close calvey cows click when they walk and move them easy or they will have early calfs that are weak cows that have enough to eat will be laying down by mid mourning if they are up feeding all day you have to many in that field if you try to hurry with a bunch of cows and calfs you just make the job longer you cant drive the drag over the top of the leaders let the drag alone and they will string out let the dogs walk out in front of you horse they have to eat less dust that way and you save them a little bit if you get lost in the mountains just let your horse have his head he knows where camp is just a few of the things i was learning when i got to stay home from school

Cow Camp Hash

1 pound hamburger
2 red potatoes
1 onion
Garlic to taste
Worcestershire sauce to taste

Brown hamburger, add onions and garlic and potatoes, salt and
pepper and Worcestershire sauce.
Cover and cook till potatoes are done

*When your in camp always burn the egg shells. It keeps the dogs from
learning to suck eggs.*

Cowboy Spaghetti

6 slices bacon
1 onion chopped
Minced garlic
Spaghetti noodles

Boil noodles and drain
Cut bacon in pieces and fry. Add chopped onion and garlic. Cook till
there about half done. Add cooked noodles and stir.

*Guys will put up with long hours, cold weather and cranky horses if you
have a good cook and feed them good.*

How Lincoln Used to be

when i was a kid lincoln was alot different than it is now it was between 3 and 5 thousand people and they all knew each other pretty much the biggest employer was the pottery and the only bank was bank of america most of the country people either farmed or ranched it was a whole different time if you needed a new pickup you went to leavall chevrolet and talked to art and he ordered you what you needed and then he carried the paper himself so you made your car payment once a year when you sold your calfs same thing with jansons you ordered next winters feed and payed in the fall after the calfs were sold east avenue grocery store also ran charge accounts but i dont know if you paid them after you sold your calfs or not same thing with the drs office alot of people that lived in our neighborhood milked a few cows and had jobs also some raised fruit and gardens and sold it in town thats how alot of the small places got paid for now lincoln has grown and has alot more people and the whole culture has changed they say its progress but i wish it was like it used to be

My First Big Horse

after rideing ponys for about 3 years I graduated to a full sized horse and boy was she a dandy a light sorrel with a strip down her face my dad had bought her at the saleyard when she was a four year old and not even halter broke she was sure snorty when he got her home but got gentle real fast and she loved us kids pop rode her for four years and when I was 8 I got her a kid couldent have gotten a better horse and I thought she was the best horse in the world grandpa hired a cowboy from Nevada he was an older man named tom mcknight and he was a hell of a horseman as well as a great cowboy the day he got here they didn't have any horses up for him and the next day they were going to gather and bell a bunch of cows to get ready to go to the mountains so pop told me that tom was going to have to ride my horse I was really disappointed because number one I wasent going to get to skip school and help and my horse got loaned out but it didn't do any good to whine about things so I just accepted it and went to school when I got home mom took us down to the red barn corrals where this was going on and they were just getting done my horse was tied up to the fence with toms saddle on her and I was looking her all over tom came over to me and said young feller its been along time since I have got to ride that nice of a horse thank you for loaning her to me I have never forgot him telling me that and how proud I was of my horse

Tom and the Working Girls

when I was nine years old we had a man named tom come down from Nevada and go to work for grand pa he stayed in camp with us all summer and he told us lots of stories about when Nevada was all open range I wish I had been older and asked him questions he also inspired me to go to Nevada when I got older well one day he told us that when he was fourteen years old they had a rodeo in elko and he was in the wild horse race the working girls all had box seats right down in front and the ranch women sat up in the stands no where near the working girls well tom was winning the wild horse race and all the working girls jumped up and started cheering him he said he had some explaining to do to his mother because she wanted to know how all the working girls knew what his name was

Being Mr. Bullochs Cowboy

being all of 8 years old and having a good horse I became mr bullocks cowboy mr bullock had about 50 cows and had little places all over the neighborhood he had a gray horse named pepper and 2 dogs a longhaired blue dog named ruff and a small slick haired dog named skipper ruff worked a little bit but skipper not so much he was just along for the adventure anyway mr bullock and I moved cows a lot we always got the job done after we were done mr bullock would have me up for dinner his wife alice was a real good cook and I thought that was pretty cool one day we were rideing thru his cows some of our cows were in the next field and one of our bulls was in with mr bullocks cows we decided to put him back and he was kind of onrey and wanted to fight our horses but we were getting him going tword the gate we were going to make it with him all the sudden skipper decided he was by god a cowdog and took after the bull and chased him the oppisite way we were going and down into a boggy creek the bull tried to jump the creek and landed in it and went clear under the mud but was able to come out the other side I learned some new cuss words from what mr bullock had to say to skipper and my dad had to go the next day and get our bull other than that time me and mr bullock always got our critter tho

Flipping the Teachers Off

by the time I got to fifth grade I was not doing well in school and had several different battles with school teachers I tried to be a good kid but I had quite a temper then and it got me in a lot of trouble at times my sister heard the teachers talking about flunking me and making me repeat fifth grade and told me what she heard now for me flunking was the absolute worst thing that could ever happen to anyone and just the thought of it made me furious but I just stuffed my feelings and kept on working one day I was out on the swings and as I swung I saw the teachers looking out the window at me and talking I thought to my self they are talking about how they are going to flunk me the more I swung the madder I got and pretty soon I was really on fire so I got off the swing and walked over in front of the window and made eye contact and gave them both the finger I really don't know to this day if that was worth it because I had to sit at my desk every recess and lunch hour the rest of the year but I didn't flunk fifth grade either

David

today I was reading the Marysville obituarys on line and I saw another old friend had passed away he was 92 years old so he had a great long life when I was about 7 we used to rent stubble from this man and put the first calf heifers on it in the fall for about six weeks they lost some weight and were much easier to calve out that way we used to go look dave up in the summer when he was harvesting because he was out early and home late so he was hard to get on the phone well any way we went over on dry creek where he was harvesting oats and he told my dad he could rent the stubble that fall he also asked if I wanted a ride on the harvester of course I said yes so I climbed up with him and we took off around the field after we got about halfway around he asked me if I wanted to drive it so I got in the seat and drove and he worked the header when we got back around the field I thought I was the most important kid in yuba county ive never driven a harvester since but I sure never forgot dave letting me drive that rest in peace old friend

The Bull Duram Hack

when we were small kids grandpa still hired a few guys they did chores some herded sheep and some were cowboys all these old guys were batcholors and they all drank and smoked ciggeretts most of them smoked bull duram and had what they called a bull duram hack every morning they would cough and spit for about an hour us kids thought these old guys were pretty neat and liked them so we used to follow them around the lawn hawking and spitting just like they did my mother took a dim view of this of course but we were exposed to so much of that she finely gave up on telling us not to do that and told us not to do that close to the steps where people walked

Replacement Heifers

when i was growing up everyone kept there own replacement heifers and calfed them out when the heifers were calving you looked at them several times a day and three times at night in case you had to pull one all the ranch wifes also took part in this and when the men were gone if a heifer needed help she got on the phone and started calling the other ranches wilsons might come pull a calf for us doug might pull a calf for wilsons we might pull a calf for doug everyone worked together and helped out each other thru heifer calving season just what you did then

Tom

when I was a boy the house at the red barn was vacant so this man and his wife asked grandpa about renting it this guy was in his early seventies and a thin small man and his name was tom his wife was Inez tom owned some old bobtail trucks and hauled hay and lumber and livestock and he made a living doing it now tom wasent much to drink but Inez was a pretty good drinking woman how ever tom once and awhile would get drunk on one of these occasions he went in a bar in Lincoln and ended up getting in an argument with three guys and beating the living daylites out of all three of them at the same time of course we heard about it and pop asked tom where he ever learned to fight like that tom told pop that when he was a young man he ran whiskey with Pretty Boy Floyd and John Dillinger when they started robbing banks he decided to come out to California sometimes you just cant tell about those old guys

Easy Chicken Pie

2 chicken breasts cut in pieces "small"
1 onion
Garlic
1 package frozen mixed vegetables
2 cans cream of chicken soup. Cream of anything will work.
1 tube canned biscuits

Cook chicken with onion and garlic. Add soup and vegetables.
Top with the biscuits and bake at 350 for 30 minutes or until the
biscuits are done and the chicken is bubbling.

*Chicken or fresh pork are both bad in camp and should be eatin the
first day. Beef, lamb or deer meat will keep a lot better. If you hang
them out at night and let them cool down in the air. At daylite, take
them down and roll them up in a canvas and keep them in the shade.*

Beef Roast

1 beef roast
Potatoes, onions, celery and carrots
Garlic
Salt and pepper

Poke holes in roast and insert cloves of garlic. Put on rack in a 12 inch
Dutch oven. 10 inch will also work.
Put a big coffee cup of water in the bottom of the Dutch oven.
Cook on 350 for "30 minutes per pound".
Next, cut up potatoes, onions, celery and carrots. Enough to fill in
around.
Roast 1 hour. Before the meat is done, put vegetables in and put lid
back on and it should have been on the whole time.

When meat and veggies are done, mix flour and water and stir into pan drippings for gravy.

When your looking for tracks if you wear orange or yellow lens glasses you can see them tracks a lot better.

Jim with Harley Elwood Hound

Acincho

another one of grandpas sheepherders I remember was acincho now
acincho was too old to take a band of sheep out so he worked around the
headquarters and helped lamb and feed and irrigated in the summer also
did the chores at the red barn whish was about a half mile from grandpas
house he would walk over to the red barn every morning with his dog
toby and half a dosen cats would follow him animals loved acincho and
toby at that time my parents and us lived at the red barn so he would
stop and talk to pop he always called him boy one mourning mom was
making waffles for breakfast and she invited him in for a waffle he had
never seen anything like that before and told pop boy you got fancy
hotcakes when the sheep lambed they had to be moved across this creek
on a narrow bridge and put into a bigger bunch until you had about a
thousand to make up a band then some other herder took them and
moved them to beale for the rest of the winter they always had a lot of
trouble crossing this bridge and grandpa had everyone out there to help
and they had a hard time no matter how much help they had one day no
one was around except pop and acincho to move about five hundred
ewes and lambs across the bridge acincho told pop when to be there
when pop got there acincho was drifting these sheep along comeing up
tword the bridge we was pushing the lambs along with his sheephook
and toby was going along bumping the lambs along with his nose when
they got up there acincho told pop now you just stay here and acincho
and toby will show you how to get these sheep to cross that bridge he
drifted those sheep down to that bridge and just held them there pretty
soon some of them got there lambs with them and started across he just
held them and pretty soon they all walked across the bridge every one
had its lambs with it and there was nothing not mothered up when they
got across acincho told pop now you see boy acincho and toby are smart
about this

Pike

another of grandpas employees was pike he stayed in a cabin across bear river and took care of a bunch of cows in the winter then In the spring he went to the mountains when the cows were in the mountains he went to sierra valley and helped put up the hay then he came back to gather and trail the cows out of the mountains and back to his camp for another winter this worked out pretty well except pike didn't drive and went horseback every where and also went on a bender once in a while one summer he was headed for the mountains and got to Graniteville and went in the bar and got drunk they kept playing don't fence me in on the juke box and pike said he was tired of hearing that and could they play something else they played it again and he went out to his horse and got his thirty thirty and came back in and shot the jukebox three times he got arrested and grandpa had to go get him out of jail he worked for grandpa sevral years after that and never shot up any more juke boxes

Tractor Mike

im sitting here this morning looking at my computer and got to thinking about some of the people i met on ranches one of these people was tractor mike he was a caretaker on a ranch i trapped on he lived at the shop and i used to drive by there to get in our out of the ranch so i used to stop and talk to him alot mike and i became good friends and after i got to know him i found out he used to be a biker and he told me alot of stories about his times as a biker but when i knew him if he liked you he was the biggest teddy bear of a guy you ever met one day i was there at the shop and he said its time to feed my birds he got some bread crumbs and called come here fellas and all these sparrows flew in and lit at his feet and he fed them he also had a family of deer that lived at the shop one christmas stephanie and i went to see him and she sang for him he was so pleased to think any one would do that for him when i retired i had a party at a place in town and i invited mike he came and everyone there liked him and he had a great time all the kids liked him and he loved all kids said they were the greatest gift we ever get in this lifetime after i retired i used to go see him once a week and we would sit out in front of the shop and drink coffee and visit sadly he got cancer and passed away but i think of him often

Belling Cows

when I was a kid we would start getting ready for the mountains first you had to gather all the different bunches of cows and get them in bigger bunches then you trailed them to a clover ranch north of wheatland then you vaccinated sprayed and put bells on them we used to put on 600 bells every spring and take them off every fall at that time every corrall had a walkway on the side of the chute behind the squeeze chute you filled the belling chute with cows and put a bell on each cow the kids job was to keep plenty of bells on the walkway and every second post had a tomato can nailed on top of it the other kids job was to cut pieces of baling wire about 10 inches long and keep those cans full because they put the bell on and then wired the strap down so it couldent come un buckled we used to try and do about 200 at a time after you belled the cows you sprayed them both side bellies and backs the spray then lasted about 2 months we used to start at daylite and try and get done by noon at the clover afterwords we would go to the hamburger stand in wheatland and have a cheeseburger and a rootbeer float I still remember how good those rootbeer floats were that hamburger stand is still there it has different owners but they still make good rootbeer floats

Jim W. Barrie

Packing Salt

packing salt was a job kids got because you had to lead the packhorse
now the pack horse might be an old gentle horse that was kind of an
extra horse or he might be some bronk my dad got in one of his horse
trades if he was an old gentle horse we only put 200 pounds on him if he
was an ass we started with 300 pounds now if you ever have to lead the
packhorse and I hope you don't there are several little rules and tricks to
that trade the obvious one is don't let the pack horse pass behind you
and rimfire your horse also don't let him jump on you when you cross a
creek also don't dally him up in boggy spots in case he decides to pull
back if hes one of pops trades you might need to snub him up first thing
in the mourning the first thing you learn about that useally by bad
experience is don't let him get any slack in the lead rope snub him so his
head is almost in your lap the reason for this is because if he gets enough
slack and it dosent take much he will pull back and jump ahead and come
right up in the saddle with you or strike you right out of it I have some
personal experience at this neither of the above is fun believe me after
you get him snubbed if hes on your right a hand side go the the left in a
small circle and make it bigger it might get pretty western for a bit but
youll be fine then get lined out and go some where useally after a mile or
so he will lead pretty good so on with the rest of the days work and lead
him back home

Getting to the Mountains with the Cows.

well after you got the cows belled and sprayed then if you were lucky you might get to go to the mountains and put up some fence they let the fences down in the fall and put them up in the summer because the snow would destroy them our range was big enough we just had fences on some private ground and what we wanted to keep cows out of if it had snowed enough that you couldent go early us and the cows arrived up there at the same time then you had to put the fences up and scatter the cows at the same time it wasent fun doing that when we went to the mountains we loaded up everything we needed for the summer and the dogs and horses and all the cows and went all at the same time we would beat the trucks up there they could get as far as webber lake then we would open the cabin at aharts camp and un load the bed rolls and get mom a bucket full of water then we had to leave and go unload the trucks they just had a loading chute along side the road and unloaded in the open my sister and I would hold the cows till they got unloaded and mothered up then we pushed them into coppins meadow and all of us rode back to camp mom always had the cabin cleaned and dinner ready just the beginning of summer work

Scattering Cows and Salt

after we had put the cows in coppins meadow the next job was to gather them out of coppins meadow and trail them down to where the road went to haypress camp there we cut out the pass creek cows and started them down pass creek then trailed the haypress and Lincoln valley cows to the lower end of haypress we left them there and rode back to camp if we were lucky we could get into haypress camp if not we stayed at aharts if we got into haypress we would spend two or three days putting up the horse field and gathering field fences then down to the lower end of haypress and gather the cows and get out the Lincoln valley cows and trail them to Lincoln valley that was a long day and a long ride home after you had the cows in those 3 places we went and scattered small bunches of them to all the meadows and creeks and feed pockets on our range a big bunch might be 30 pairs a small bunch might be 15 pair to keep them where you wanted them you packed salt and put it out at each place that held those cows in that area I personly think a lot of why there arnt many permits like that anymore is because people cant and don't live with there cows anymore then everyone lived with there cows

Mexican Meat Loaf

2 pounds hamburger
1 onion chopped
1 bell pepper chopped
Crushed doritos (I like nacho cheese)
1 package taco seasoning mix
1 egg

Mix everything and shape into a loaf. I use a mixing bowl. Put rack in crock pot, add meat loaf, cook on low 8 hours. Makes really good sandwiches!

A cooked roast is really handy to take to camp. There is really a lot of things you can do with it. You can make stew, sandwiches, hash. I also like to take boiled potatoes to camp. If I have room, they are very handy to have.

Stew

2 packages stew meat or chuck steak or London broil cut in small pieces
4 big potatoes cut small
2 onions chopped
2 chili peppers or bell peppers cut in small pieces
1 can tomato sauce
2 28 ounce cans diced tomatoes
Garlic to taste
One large package frozen mixed vegetables
1 28 ounce can beef broth

Brown meat in Dutch oven. Add onion, potatoes and the rest including beef broth. Bring to a boil and simmer till vegetables are done. Or, can cook in Crock pot low 8 hours.

When your looking at a horse to buy that's supposed to be broke, always look at the shoe job on him. If the nails are real uneven ask whos been shoeing him. If it's a professional horseshoer, the horse is probably hard to shoe.

Coming Out Of Lincoln Valley

when i was a kid opening weekend of deer season is when we moved the cows out of lincoln valley mom would pick us up after school and we would drive to the camp pop and jim would be up there already they stayed all fall and gathered rode lots of miles also any way we would get there and un load mom would get supper ready for when pop and jim got in the next morning we would load up before daylite and drive over to lincoln valley and unload then mom drove the truck back to camp the four of us would gather all the cows in lincoln valley and bunch them and my sister and i would hold them while pop and jim made a circle around there and made sure none had left as lincoln valley wasent fenced when they got back we started up over this steep ridge there was an old skid road going all the way to the top pop and jim always went with the leaders and nona and i brought the drag we had about three hundred pair and it was a long ways up that trail almost always it was cold and the wind was blowing hard when we broke over the top we went down log cabin canyon to haypress and into the gathering field at camp then we rode back to camp at about dark just one of my childhood memories

Shipping Calfs on the Mountain

when we went to the mountains after you got the cows gathered and put in the gathering field at haypress and pushed into jones valley then we trailed the haypress cows to aharts camp and brought the cows from jones valley to aharts that place had a good fence around it and corralls and scales the only corralls on the whole range then the calf buyer got called and you set a date to ship this entailed a trip tp sierraville to the pay phone so while we were down there we told the wilson bros and the leavell bros when we were going to ship the morning of shipping day everyone got to aharts way before daylight and we rode to the back of the field as soon as you could see we started drifting those cows tword the corralls you always move cattle easy to the scales because after a whole years work its payday when they got in the corrals we sorted the cows off the calfs and sorted the calfs heifers and steers and weighed them then the buyer went to find the trucks and bring them in to load on year the trucks came in on there own and took a wrong turn and ended up on a log landing the loggers shut the job down and hooked the cat on the trailers and got them turned around there were eight sets of doubles then we loaded the calfs and sent them on there way one year it snowed about a foot and pop had to got down to sierra valley and buy a truckload of hay and feed every thing and we shiped in the snow again some loggers sent a cat to pull the trucks away from the chute and up a little hill those guys were great and everyone in those mountains worked together we bought that crew a half gallon of whisky for that mom always had a big meal during shiping for who ever were there the year it snowed everyone got to makeing snow cones out of early times and the brand inspector really got plastered so one of the wilsons drove him home and the other one drove the state car home for him the loggers that were there for lunch behaved and so did everyone else after the cows quit bawling they trailed them down to sierra valley till it rained down here

Tracks

when we went to the mountains when you gathered and also all summer you spent alot of time looking for and at tracks because of the timber you couldent see like you can in other places and you have to track cows alot we also belled all the cows to make it easyer to find them but you spent alot of time tracking cows when we were really small pop taught us to tell old tracks from fresh tracks and as we grew he was always testing us by asking if we saw any tracks and how freash were they this useally happened when we were rideing along and if you hadent noticed the tracks you were garentied an ass chewing the reason he did this is because when we got old enough to go on our own we wouldent come home and tell him we saw fresh tracks someplace and then he would ride all the way down there with the dogs and have them be old tracks by the time we were nine or ten we were pretty good trackers you always hoped for a rain about two thirds of the way thru gathering because any track you saw after the rain was a fresh track all those mountain guys were good trackers they all used dogs and your dogs would start to smell tracks and trail cows this early training sure came in handy when i got started trapping the first time i went with the federal trapper he sent me down this creek while he checked some traps when he picked me up he asked me if i had seen anything i told him no but there were fresh coyote tracks in there after that he took me with him alot and showed me alot of things i would never have got to learn otherwise

How I learned to Cook

when we were kids mom did all the cooking and pop ran the ranch outside one time we were in the mountains and mom had to come home for a few days so pop was going to do the cooking for him and me and my sister to say that pop wasn't much of a cook would be an understatement for breakfast we got scorched eggs and burned bacon lunch wasn't bad it was sandwiches then came supper he took leftover gravy and caned creamed corn and caned sardines and made soup out of it I still can remember the taste of it when mom got back I told her I wanted to learn to cook so the next time she left I could be the cook so the next morning she started me cooking eggs and bacon and ive been cooking ever since altho now I cook sometimes as stephanie does most of the cooking

When Pop Ate the Dog Food

the last story was about cooking this story is along the same lines when we were teenagers pop got pretty bad to drink for a few years thankfully he quit drinking and was sober the rest of his life but for a few years it was pretty bad and mom sure didn't think much of it either around our house mom served supper at six oclock and unless you were still out working if you missed supper you were on your own this one night pop was off getting a snoot full and we ate supper and went to bed mom always kept a potfull of scraps and leftovers on the back of the stove for the dogs we fed them everyday so they were always fresh well pop came home after drinking quite a bit and thought mom had left that out for him and heated up a bowl full for himself mom remembered that the rest of her life and laughed about it I don't imagine pop thought it was to funny but the rest of us sure did

Reds Fried Trout

Trout. We used to catch 8 to 10 inch.
Corn meal
Slices of garlic
Bacon grease

Roll fish in corn meal, put slice of garlic inside and fry in bacon grease.

Red was a guy I worked with at A in Nevada. He was an older man and to put it mildly, he had a drinking problem. One day he helped me tie a horse down and shoe him. I told him I would buy him a bottle of whiskey, what kind did he want. He said Jim Beam. I said I'd buy him better whiskey than that he said no it comes in a square bottle and they don't roll under my bed so I don't have to get up and find them under the bed at nite when I want a drink.

Canned Tamales and Chicken

2 chicken breast cut up small
1 onion
Garlic
3 or 4 cans hormell tamales
1 can cream of mushroom soup, 26 ounces

Cook chicken in Dutch oven with garlic and onions.
Open tamales and make sure to get the paper off them.
Add them and the juice to the chicken. Add the cream of mushroom soup and bake at 350 till bubbly. You can also add cheese on top.

When you sight your rifle in, you should do it over several days. No more than 2 shots at a time. That way, you get it zeroed with a cold barrel. If you fire it several times, the barrel is hot. You might have it where you want it then. After the barrel cools, it might shoot somewhere else entirely.

Bud

by 1971 the mountains were getting harder to deal with they had so
many roads up there that cows didn't stay in places like they used to so
my parents were pretty disgusted also that summer our camp burned
down so the decision was made to go to sierra valley they had been going
down there in the fall for 2 years they rented a place from a guy named
bud out by loyalton the next spring when we shipped to sierra valley I got
to meet bud he was a Nevada buckaroo all the way spade bit bridle horse
single rig saddle and a long rope and he was pretty handy I thought the
first day we moved cows up there we had a roan bull that was really
mean and would fight your horse we were trying to put him and some
cows out of a field and he got on the fight bud roped him and jerked the
daylights out of him he went thru the gate and before anybody could
heel him bud rode around him and wraped his hind feet up and layed him
down and dave got his rope off dave worked for bud and he wanted to
learn to ride bucking horses they had a bucking barrell set behind the
bunkhouse and rode it every nite of course I had to try it after they
bucked me off about three times bud showed me how to move my feet
and lift up on my reins after that I did better I was already thinking I
wanted to be like bud but about three weeks later we had a bull get in
the neighbors and we were getting him out and going to bring him down
to Lincoln so he didn't get in there again we had him in the corrall and the
guy that worked for the neighbor came by and started bitching about our
bull pop told him we were takeing him home but he just kept bitching
about our bull bud was standing there and told that guy if that's the way
you feel I will get over the fence and kick the daylights out of you after I
was hooked and all I thought of was being a buckaroo

Sale Yard Job

when i was sixteen we had a bunch of yearlings at a feedlot up by
marysville and we sold them so a guy from roseville auction came up to
ship them and he told my parents if i wanted a job to come down to the
sale it was one day a week on saterdays so pop told me to take it and i
would learn about a sale yard the next saterday i went down to the sale
yard and i didnt have enough sense to go to the office so i went down to
the unloading dock and stood around there until the boss asked me what
i wanted i replied a job and he said do you promise to show up on
saterdays im tired of hireing a bunch of damed kids that dont show up i
said i would be there every saterday he gave me a whip and paired me up
with another kid to start penning cattle after i had worked about three
hours the assistant manager came out there and asked me if i had gone
to the office and filled out the paperwork and punched the time clock
and i told him no i thought you got paid by the month and what
paperwork he said this was different than ranches and to come with him
we went to the office and i had to show my social security card and then
he told the book keeper this boy has worked on ranches his whole life
and never worked anywhere like this before he started three hours ago
vern the book keeper said ok i will write his time down and then he
showed me how to write my name on a time card and put it in the time
clock and told me when i was done for the day i had to punch out thats
the story of my first job interview and experience working in town

Herding Turkeys

i thought i would tell you some stories my dad told me it seems like
everyone is into history pop told me when he was a boy every ranch
raised a flock of turkeys some had hens and raised the turkeys from
chicks others bought chicks and raised them when they got big enough

pop and his brother herded them all summer around on the creeks and where ever else they could find some thing for them to eat thats where pop learned to train herding dogs pop told me along in the fall late september or early october the turkey buyer came around and bought these farm flocks and put them together and made a flock of around 3000 they drove those turkeys from place to place until they got enough then they drove them over to the west side of the sacramento valley because they raised alot of dryland grain over there those old harvesters lost alot of grain so those big bunches of turkeys fed those stubble field and ate the grain the harvesters lost around november they ended up down around petaluma where there was a big turkey processing plant and were processed for thanksgiving and christmas when i was real little i remember going over to sheridan and crossing the highway and going down dowd road and someone pop knew was driveing a bunch of turkeys down the county road but thats the only time i ever saw anything like that

Pop Stops the Train

this is another story my dad told me he didnt tell me this one till i was about 45 years old pop quit school when he was a sophmore and went to work for his uncle herding sheep when it got spring him and an old man named bob ogdon drove those sheep from where beale air force base is to cisco grove up on interstate 80 thats where the sheep summered he told me when they started out the camped the first night on rock creek and the next morning the pack horse bucked the pack off and made a huge mess of all there food and everything else so they moved on when they got up around colfax they had to camp early one day and herd the sheep along the railroad pop told me that bob had made him a walking stick to kill snakes with and he was between the sheep and the railroad tracks keeping the sheep off the tracks and there were alot of blobs of grease that were laying along the tracks he started jabbing them with his stick and smearing them on the rails because he was bored he did that all afternoon that evening when they were in camp fixing supper the train came along and pop said all the sudden it made all kinds of roaring and funny sounds and stoped bob asked pop billy what did you to to the track pop told him about the grease bob told him that train cant get traction and there going to have to send a crew out to sand the tracks if the railroad guys come over here to camp and ask us anything about it dont say anything the rail road didnt come to there camp and the next day they moved on tword the mountains

The Horse Traders

another story pop told me was one his dad told him was before the goldfields on the yuba river were started the yuba river made a bend there and there was always grass and shade and the horse traders camped there so if you wanted a horsetrade you went down there and took what you had to trade and looked at what the traders had to trade the traders always tried to get your horse and something besides they called that boot if he was a good trader he might have collected boot when he traded for that horse and collect boot when he traded that horse to you these traders would start in southern california and trade there way up into oregon and washington and then back down thru california to where ever they started from they always tried to trade for the kind of horses someone might at the next stop pop told me some of those old guys were still around when he was a kid and you sure could learn something from them i guess thats why pop was always kind of a horse trader

Grandpa Boarding Teams

my dad told me that after grandpa and grandma got married he rented a ranch over by the goldfields and it was a pretty good sized place and he would take in freight teams for the winter and run them on the native grass when the snow melted and the freighting got busy again the owners of those teams would send word to grandpa when they wanted them he would get them in and start graining them every day and drive them hitched up to three emtey wagons hooked together pop told me he would get them to where they trotted out ten miles and turned around and came back then he shod them all most were ten horse teams then the owners came and picked them up and started freighting i guess in that day that was a pretty good business i wish i had of been older when grandpa was healthy enough to tell me about doing things like that over in the spenceville wild life area there is the remains of the town of spenceville there is a cement bridge there with a date of 1900 or 01 and when they finished that grandpa was the first one to cross it with a freight team

The Appy Colt

there is an old saying there never was a horse that couldent be rode or a cowboy that couldent be throwed this story is along those lines when i was fourteen we rented a ranch in sierra valley and i met bud he was from nevada and showed me alot of things including how to ride a bucking horse he put me on a bucking barrell and coached me about how to move my feet and sit up we had some colts we had bought that liked to buck and i was rideing them and getting them rode everytime they tried me i thought i was pretty damed forked to say the least my mother had raised an appy colt out of her favorite mare and we hauled her up there for me to start now at that time i had no idea how to start a colt

51

properly so i just saddled her up and let her buck with the saddle and drove her around till she was bridle wise about an hour and got on her and rode her she didnt buck so i thought i had her pretty broke the next day mom went out to watch me ride her colt and i saddled her up and un tracked her and steped on her and moved her off she took about ten steps and bogged her head and my god could she buck i rode her across the corrall and she bucked me off and just drove my head in the dirt she skined me from above my eye to the bottom of my jaw and gave me a huge black eye also i came away from that little lesson realising that i couldent ride all of them and its better to take your time and not let them horses buck and also never show some a colt on his second ride just the thing every fourteen year old boy needs to have happen to teach humility

Mexican Steak

3 pounds chuck steak cut in strips
2 onions
4 chili peppers mild or 2 bell peppers
2 spoons minced garlic
1 28 ounce can diced tomatoes
3 Tablespoons chili powder
Ground cumin to taste

Put some olive oil in Dutch oven. Add meat, onions and peppers.
Brown meat.
Add tomatoes and chili powder and cumin. Simmer till done. You can
serve this like it is or with rice or make fajitas or enchiladas out of it.

Enchilada Sauce

2 cans tomato sauce
2 cans water
4 Tablespoons chili powder
1 spoon minced garlic
Mix together and simmer 10 minutes

Enchiladas

Corn tortillas
2 pounds hamburger
1 onion
Chili peppers to taste, canned or fresh
1 spoon minced garlic
Grated chedder cheese or pepper jack

Brown hamburger, add onion and garlic.
Cook till done in Dutch oven or casserole pan
Spoon some sauce on bottom. Layer tortillas, then meat and some sauce and cheese. Add another layer of tortillas. Cover with sauce and cheese.
Bake at 350 till cheese melts and it bubbles. You can make as many layers as you like.

When your calling coyotes and you call 2 and shoot the first one and the other one runs off a lot of times if you keep calling the one that ran of will come back to see about his partner.

How Cold It Gets In Sierra Valley

this morning ed and i were comparing stories about how cold it can get in sierra valley here are two experiances i had along those lines when we were still going to the mountains we sent cows to sierra valley in the spring until we could get on the forest service we had those cows out of sattley in a place they call the mounds pop and i were up there looking at the cows one day it was a buetiful day no wind and warm great weather about ten oclock in the morning the clouds blew in and it started pouring rain and then it turned to hail about the size of marbels we were along ways from the truck and we hit a lope for the truck but we sure got beat up before we got there and got our horses loaded the dogs were so beat up and cold we put them in the cab with us i dont know if we could have made it if we didnt have the truck to go back to the next experiance was when we ran cows out by loyalton pop had came up and we gathered all the cows and cut out all the calvey cows and were going to ship them home and just leave pairs up there we did that every year so the calfs were older when you had to ship them it sure made it easyer well we started tword the corralls with about three hundred cows we had to go about three miles to the corralls same thing the weather was buetiful then the north wind came up and blew a snowstorm in we had those cows out on a dirt road fenced on both sides we were freezing driveing those cows along and our neighbor frank saw us and came in his pickup and followed the cows one of us would get in with frank and get warmed up and the other one would drive the cows and lead the other guys horse we just kept switching back and forth like that all the way to the corralls thank god for great neighbors also two days i wouldent want to repeat

Jim W. Barrie

Fall in the Sierra Valley

this week we had 2 days that felt like fall in the mornings it reminded me of when we had cows in sierra valley i stayed up there from august till december by myself and took care of six hundred cows i started doing that when i was seventeen i had to keep all the cows pushed across the river and go get the pairs as they calfed and bring them back across the river to a hay field by the house also calf out some first calf heifers and take care of anything else that came up the house we lived in didnt have electricity or running water it had and arteisan well in the front yard and the pipe came out of the well and teed one way went to a water trough and the other way went into this old bath house if you wanted to take a bath you turned the water off going to the trough and it ran into the bath tub the water was luke warm and felt pretty good in the summer but about november takeing a bath was quite an experiance i used to get a big bucket of water and put it on the cookstove and get it boiling and fill the bath tub while my water on the stove was getting hot then pour the boiling water in and take a bath i also used to plan my day so i could do this about three oclock in the afternoon when it was the warmest part of the day you sure didnt do any long soaks in the tub either sometimes when i would cross the river and bring pairs out of there the water would be frosen and i would have trouble with those cows with baby calfs if i was lucky when i got up to the ice if i got off and led my horse i could grab one of those small calfs and shove him out on the ice and his mother would chase him out on the ice and break it then i would get back on my horse and drive the rest of the pairs across it didnt take me long to figure out to go three times a week so i didnt have very big bunches to cross with if that didnt work some times i would have to get a small bunch of calvey cows and cross them to break the ice that water would splash up on your overshoes and freeze before it could run off but i was liveing my dream of becomeing a buckaroo

56

Pasole

2 pounds pork cut in cubes
1 large onion
6 sweet wax or mild chili peppers or can use 1 large bell pepper. Cut in slices or cubes
1 can enchilada sauce "red", 12 ounce
1 can tomato sauce, 12 ounce
3 spoon fulls chili powder
1 box chicken stock
Minced garlic to taste
2 cans hominy, drained

Brown meat, chop onions and peppers.
Mix enchilada sauce, tomatoe sauce, chicken stock, garlic and chili powder. Stir till combined.
Put in a slow cooker, add hominy and cook on low 8 hours.

While your doing todays meal if you do tomorrows prep work it will sure save some time.

Salsa

3 large tomatoes
6 green chili peppers
1 large onion
Minced garlic
Splash of vinegar
Sprinkle of oregano and cumin

Chop onion and peppers together. Slice tomatoes and add then chop the whole mess and add vinegar, garlic, cumin and oregano. Also salt and pepper to taste.

*** Your peppers will regulate how hot this is. I use really mild pepper. You can add siracha pepper paste if you want it hotter.

Grandpa Barrie Freighting

lee showed me some pictures of the covered bridge over the yuba river
when grandpa barrie was 9 his father took him and his brother out of
school and put them to work farming by the time grandpa was twelve he
and uncle jack and there dad were freighting from marysville to the
mountain towns and they all were driveing ten horses pulling three
wagons they would haul groceries out of marysville across the covered
bridge up tp the small towns in the mountains and ceder shakes back to
marysville can you imagine a twelve year old crossing that bridge with ten
horses and three wagons hooked together then going up the grades to
those towns also comeing out of there with loaded shakes those guys
were tough i also have a picture here in the house of grandpa when he
was sixteen driveing 32 horses and mules on a harvester on the other
side of the family granda churchs family used to cross that bridge with six
hundred cows and there calfs every spring going to the mountains and
cross comeing back home also just thought i would share my connection
to the covered bridge

Buck

as ive told you before grandpa had over the years several different
employees some herded sheep some were cowboys most worked thru
the spring and summer and got layed off after the cows were home and
scattered old buck was one of these buck had grown up around this area
but he had a wandering streak to him and had done quite a few different
things one was he drove a twenty mule team out of death valley hauling
borax when he worked for grandpa he was hired as a cowboy and he was
a good one he worked here several years part time one day him and my
dad were gathering cows up where hidden falls park is now there was an
old tumble down house there and he told pop that when he was young

he was married and lived in that house apparently he and his wife didn't get along very well and one night he woke up and she was just pulling down on him with a thirty thirty he went out the window before she could shoot and went down to Bakersfield and went to work for miller and lux after a few years he came back to this country I don't know if he and his wife tried again or not when we were small he stayed at haypress camp with us I can remember watching him peel an onion and eat it like and apple he had a big buckskin horse he called rawhide and a dog he called dot we thought dot was really neat because she liked kids and shook hands he also was quite a drinking man and every summer he would tell pop he needed to go to auburn and renew his drivers license pop would get him a ride on a logging truck down to auburn and he would go on a bender for a few days then come back up on another logging truck and be good for the rest of the summer and fall then mom and us would take him and his bed roll and saddle to loomis and he would stay with his brother and sister in law till the next spring every time he saw us kids if he hadn't seen us in a while he gave us each a silver dollar I still have mine finely he got old and went to Nevada and was a care taker on a small ranch till he passed away

Pop Getting Bucked off in the River

when we started going to sierra valley we lived right where the feather river started it was a big swamp with high ground scattered all thru it we had to keep the cows pushed across the river so about twice a week my dad and my sister and me would cross about 300 pair one particular day we were doing that and things wernt going well pop was mad at the world the dogs wernt working good the cows didn't want to start across and according to pop my sister and I couldent do any thing right either he was bitching us out all mourning finley we got them to start across now the river had a solid bottom and the water was about four feet deep but half was just black slimey stinking mud from decaying tules and after we crossed cow manure we got a everything going across and followed them just a little way out in that mess and pop saw a duck decoy and rode over to it and started to pick it up he was rideing a brown mare to got on a trade that spring that we was pretty high on when he picked up the decoy it had string on the bottom and it had wraped around his horses leg she moved and the decoy followed she got scared and bucked pop off in that slime and he sailed out thru the air and landed right in that mess and went clear under his horse ran off and my sister and I had to go catch her we sure laughed while we caught his horse but made sure we wernt still laughing when we got back

My First Fall in Sierra Valley

when we went to sierra valley I was fourteen and we ended up staying there for seven years summer there winter down here I still didn't do well in school and was quickly learning some pretty rowdy ways also all I thought of was being a buckaroo and going to Nevada as soon as I could anyway I made it thru high school and didn't end up in juvenile hall or some other place as soon as I graduated we went to sierra valley for the summer and along about august pop told me him and mom and my sister were going back down below to get ready to start buying cattle to run thru the winter and I was to take of the cows and calf out about 60 first calf heifers I was supposed to go into town once a week and call home so they would know that I hadn't drowned crossing the river they didn't have cell phones then and our house didn't have running water or electricity man what a culture shock to be on my own with six hundred cows to take care of I had to keep them pushed across the river and go across the river every other day and get the pairs and cross them and take them to a hayfield also go thru those heifers at least twice a day and get any that needed help in and pull the calfs I was one busy fellow and it sure kept me out of mischief I was pretty much over my head at first but I hung in there and kept going and got it done after that first fall I really looked forward to being up there by myself in the fall

Green Beans with Tomatoes

1 package frozen green beas
1 or 2 cans diced tomateos
6 slices bacon cut small
Minced garlic
1 small onion chopped small

Fry bacon, add onion. Cook. Add to beans, add tomatoes and garlic.
Cook till everything simmers.

Cowboy Cole Slaw

Sliced carrots, fresh
Sliced celery, fresh
Chopped onion
Salad dressing
Mix and serve

Salad Dressing

2/3 cup oil (I like olive oil)
½ cup vinegar
Mustard, Dijon or regular
Minced garlic
Italian seasoning, dry or fresh.

Mix oil, vinegar and mustard. The mustard keeps it from separating.
Add garlic and spices to taste. The sky is the limit.

When you go to camp always take a small cheap sewing kit. It comes in handy. Also, a pair of cheap vice grips is really handy.

Frank and Howard

after we ran cows in sierra valley for seven years the ranch changed hands and my parents sold the cows and started buying cattle and running them thru the winter down here and I had the summers to find something to do that first summer I went back to sierra valley and started colts with two phenominal horsemen frank and howard frank was an older man and howard was his son they had about 45 head of big waspy colts off the desert to start and howard and I started them now these horses were well bred horses but they sure had some sting and action I had never rode colts like that before so it was quite a learning curve howard would look you right in the eye and tell he couldent ride them bronks well and I don't know if he could have rode one in a rodeo but out in the open he could ride one as well as anyone I ever saw before or since I sure learned a lot that summer things I still use today fourty years later also frank was a truly great bridel man and I learned a lot from him that I still use today I guess what im trying to say is that summer was the best investment of my time I ever spent and greatest gift I ever got

Riding Broncos

Ive told you about rideing broncos for frank and howard they were from central Nevada and the first thing they told me was we don't call it rideing colts its starting broncos the first mourning I was there howard caught me this horse they called john barnes he was a horse howard was starting for someone else and really pretty gentle I saddled him up and howard told me to get on him in the round corall I rode him around the round corrall three laps each way and frank let me out on him and howard said lets go out and check some steers we started out and john grabbed his ass and started to run off I pulled back on both reins and he really got scared howard shot past me and yelled pull one rein so I got him stoped the howard spent about half an hour showing me how to double a horse and told me if you cant get one stoped in a hundred feet or less just pitch him his head and enjoy the ride well after that experience I never learned how to enjoy the ride but I became an expert at getting one doubled and shut down in a hundred feet or less

Tapedero

after about two weeks of rideing john barnes and a mare howard owned named Maryetta she was a bridel horse and a good one the first time I rode her I got on her like I was climbing thru a barn window and she almost bucked me off howard told me I scared her and showed me how to get on a horse by turning my stirrip and steping on one day he caught a bay six year old gelding and told me to saddle him and take him to the round pen and run him around some then he came out and said I will get on him and un track him for you he did and then he had me watch how he got on him and told me he was funny to get on I later learned if someone told you that a horse was funny you better dam sure watch him he told me to get on him so I did and rode him around the round pen howard said lets go move the steers to another field we went and did that took us a couple hours and this horse was great and I got along with him real good when we got back to the barn and unsaddled howard told me im going to tell you this because your doing really good other than me your the first guy to even make it on that horse after I got over being scared I was pretty proud of myself I rode that horse for about a month before he sold and always really got along with him

Hobbling Them Broncos

after we got the started and broke horses sold we started on the unstarted horses we would catch each one and tie them up for a while then take them to the round corrall and get them in the middle of it and hobble there front feet with sack hobbles after they tried those hobbles we put sack hobbles on there hind feet and tied them to the frount hobbles they didn't useally throw themselves but they sure learned to stand hobbled then we crawled all over them they didn't sack them out with a saddle blanket they said crawling on and around them was better after a bit of crawling on them we saddled them up and tied a rope to the end of the halter rope so you stay out of the way better and un hobbled them useally they just kind of froze there until you moved them the idea was to keep them from bucking a lot of times you could but sometimes they really came undone and would buck out to the end of that rope and when you jerked on it they would come right at you bucking that's why the longer halter rope after you got them calmed down you put a snaffle bit in their mouths and tied it up to the brow band and sent them around the round corrall and started steping in frount of them and turning them into the fence when they turned you hurry them out of the turn so they learned to turn and jump out at the same time they said that was very important to teach them forward motin if they got scared and started running off you just kept steping in frount of them and turning them back till they slowed down or stoped this was all before ray hunt and those horsemen were very well known frank and howard were truly way ahead of there time after a few days of that you hobbled them and got on and off them then un hobbled them and drove them so they learned to be bridle wise tomorrow the first ride

First Ride on Them Broncos

this story is about the first ride on the horses at frank and howards after you could get on and off them they were ready to ride now most of those horses were at least half thourobred and they were sensitive also we used to ride them in a halter the first ride you I was always nervous about the first ride and asked frank and howard all kinds of questions about how to go about it there advice was take command of him and ride him like your own horse and don't worry about the ground until you hit it makes sense now but not much to go on then after you saddled them you would untrack them in the round corrall then hobble them and get on and off a couple times then take the hind hobbles off and un tie the front hobbles but leave them around his legs then get on him and ride him out of the hobbles then they wanted you to hit a trot and go around once each way then gallop him if they wouldent gallop get down your quirt and move him out i used to hate hearing get down your quirt and move him out after you galloped them each way they wanted you to swing you rope on them I had never done anything this way before but im hear to tell you if you swing a rope the first ride you wont ever have an issue with it the next day was the same and the third day you untracked them and turned them once each way and went outside

Sit Down and Hang On

above we covered the first ride after 2 days in the round corrall we went outside on those horses howard would ride his right out thru the loose horses I useally went down a dirt road that went by the house you could trot down it about 5 miles and come back if you wanted to go across the ranch you could go in the field and thru the fields back home these horses were really sensitive ive never rode horse like them since if you tiped ones nose one way or the other and layed your rein against there neck they acted like that rein was red hot once you got a few rides on them they were truly a pleasure to ride how ever they were firery hot buggers and would sure run away with you one day I was in a field and had a horse I called pardner run away with me he ran all the way across the field and right up to a six wire fence and turned after I got him stoped I saw frank out on the road in his pickup watching me when I got in that afternoon frank was at the barn and said partner ran away with you huh I said yes he scared the crap out of me frank said why I said I thought he was going to run thru the fence with me frank replied when one of my horses runs up to a fence like that sit down and hang on hes going left or right I don't own any dumb enough to go thru the fence

First Day on the Circle A

after six months with frank and howard it was time to come home and work thru the winter and spring so after that I was looking for a job again I called around for a job starting colts but didn't have any luck a friend told me a guy I knew was managing the quarter circle a in paradise valley Nevada so I called him he said to come on up the first day I got there he told me I would be staying at the ranch and helping him a few days so the next morning at breakfast I met 2 of the guys from camp red and chuck they were going to help us also gary caught me a sorrel horse named alby red told me to watch him as he sure might buck a guy off I saddled him in the barn and he really humped up so we loaded our horses in a gooseneck and went down the road a few miles when we un loaded alby was still humped up pretty bad they had just resurfaced the road and the pavement was really slippery I figured alby was smart enough to not buck on that slick pavement so I got on him right in the middle of the road and rode him down it a ways and crossed the bar pit he was fine after that and we gathered a bunch of steers and moved them I guess I passed the test with gary because he sent me out to camp with red and chuck that afternoon

CowPuncher Salad

Canned tomatoes
Onions
Canned chili peppers
Splash of vinegar
Combine and serve

From Arizona they often have to take food to camp on pack mules

Fried Potatoes

6 red potatoes quartered and sliced
1 large onion quartered and sliced
Olive oil
Minced garlic

Quarter and slice potatoes and rinse. Put olive oil in pan, get hot, add potatoes. Cover and fry. When they are about half done, add onions and garlic. Finish cooking.

Cowboy Potato Salad

Take leftover fried potatoes and left over bacon. Chop bacon, add to potatoes. Maybe also some fresh onion, sweet pickles and mustard and mayonnaise. Stir and chill.

When you go to camp, boiled potatoes are always handy to have. You can fry, mash, add them to stew, anything.

Shoeing Wills Packer

after we got out to camp it was just getting tword supper time I unloaded
my bedroll and saddle and alby we had hauled him out for me to ride
after I turned alby loose I met the rest of the crew there was blane the
cowboss and dave and kelly kellys wife was also there cooking they didn't
run a wagon and worked out of camps this camp was Kelly creek is had a
pretty good house made out of railroad ties and a few trees around it
there was an emty tepee tent so I moved my stuff in there everybody
wanted to know where in California I came from because gary had hired
some guys from California that were team roper types and they couldent
cut it they couldent figger out why I had a single rig saddle and a long
rope and no rubber on my horn the next morning blane caught me a
sorrel flaxen maned horse and said this is willis packer hes hard to get on
and you will have to tie him down to shoe his hind feet use your snaffle
bit on him now willis had been around a few owners because he had
several different brands on him I took him over and tied him up and
hobbled him and saddled him we hauled out that day so when we
unloaded I put my bridel on willis and cinched him up good and gathered
him up good and steped on him he tried to jump away but I kept him
from doing it after that I just left him alone and we got along fine we
worked that country and one day we had a short day blane said what are
we going to do this afternoon I said im going to shoe willis packer behind
he said I want a front row seat for that I said your going to get one
because ive never tied a horse down to shoe him and your going to have
to help blane just laughed and said if your honest enough to tell me that I
will help you red also said he would help so that afternoon we tied willis
down and put hind shoes on him I made my mind up then before I left
there I would shoe him standing up and I did the next weekend we went
to town on saterday night and blane told me to come by the gem bar and
he would buy me a drink so I went in there we were setting at a table and

some guy at the bar got ignorant with the bartender the bartender jumped right over the bar and grabbed that guy buy the coller and his belt and ran him across the room and opened the door with his head and thru him out in the gutter blane said you just saw ray give a basque flying lesson

Bullhead Ranch

while I was at the quarter circle a there were all kinds of neat things to see especialy for a guy from California on the way out to little humbolt there was a place called bullhead ranch it had a great big house and some out buildings all made of sandstone blocks these blocks were cut square and were soft we all scratched our names and dates in them it was real interesting reading the names of other buckaroos who worked there over the years another neat thing at little humbolt they had a big willow corrall we caught horses in they set posts in the ground about 2 feet apart every 8 feet and filled the space up with willows they made good corrals but you have to put more willows on them every year it also will keep you from leaning on them because rattlesnakes like to crawl up in them and hide also they had big high rims around there and they only had trails going down thru them blane knew all those trails so we used to cut thru the rims on our way back to camp as you rode down those trail you would see rattlesnakes sticking there heads up thru the rocks ahead of you and then have to ride over them no one ever got bit or nobodys horses did either

Things I Saw at Circle A

while we were camped at little humbolt we were rideing way out tword the il and ellisons and came across a monument there had been a guy named jack frusetta and he was rideing across the desert going over to rep for quarter circle a but one of the early owners Im just repeting what was told to me here any some how he broke his leg and his horse got away the horse showed up some where and it took a few days to figger things out they back tracked him and found him dead where that monument stands today he had crawled several miles before he died it was a pretty sobering ride that day and hearing that story another day we were out at a place they called rodeer flats blane told me when he was a kid three separate wagons met there and worked that country he said the kids got the job of day herding the horses it was the worst job you could imagine he said because every time you looked horses were trying to leave and go back to which ever ranch they belonged to just a couple things I thought I would share

The Mustangs

well after the trip to town we got word to move to little humbolt camp and move some cows back to the mountains and gather a bunch of heifers and move them across the desert to rock springs pasture there were around 2000 of these heifers and they were all brahma cross a real pretty bunch we got them gathered and started for rock springs the north wind was blowing hard and these heifers were strung out for a long ways when we came to button lake there were a bunch of wild horses watering there and bunches of horses scattered as far as you could see waiting to come and drink the bunch that was drinking got scared and ran thru the next bunch and they all got confused and started running back and forth and mixing with other bunches there were sevral hundred horses mixed and they ran back and forth in frount of us sevral times then they got about a half mile from us and the studs started cutting there mares out we just let the heifers go to the lake and watched for about an hour it truly was one of the greatest things I ever got to watch

Kitty

when I worked on the circle a we went thru a lot of help and it included cooks first we had kellys wife but she and kelly moved on then we had dorethy then she got a better job and then we had terrys wife she was a real good cook but their kids were starting school so we were between cooks and I was also cooking as well as rideing the ranch cook was a guy named jack and he had quite a gig going for himself he had a wife and kids in town so he had her get on welfare and tell them he abandoned them and then he was going in to see her and takeing groceries and telling gary he was sending them out to camp so we were almost starving one evening we went down to the ranch and resupplied our selfs and gary came along and caught us and asked us what we were doin after about an hour long conversation everyone figured out what jack was up to and gary fired him a few days later greg and I went down to the ranch and gary was all smiles and said I tried to get dorethy back and she wanted to come back but shes not available till 2 weeks from now but I found another lady she is great so we met kitty she was one of the most disagreeable people I ever met and by the time we got out to camp she was on the warpath about everything we got her settled in the cabin and went to bed the rest of the crew were already in bed the next morning I heard blane get up and when he went by my tent he said roll out so I got dressed and sat on the edge of my bed just to see what was going to happen in about three minuts he came tearing back out and said whos that old barracuda and where in the hell did she come from I explaned that that was our new cook and gary said she was really going to mother us blane said the way she snarled at me when I walked in there I don't see that happening we all went to the cabin and kitty demanded to be taken to the ranch so I hauled her back down there and told gary I would gladly keep cooking for the crew till dorethy could come back

Andy and Terry

after the big rain when we moved the heifers we got started gathering in ernest before we could ride the waters and find a lot of cows after that they were scattered all over out there you find bunches of three or four pairs instead of bunches of fifty or sixty blane decided to split the crew and he made me jigger boss and gave me terry andy and an indian kid named Myron they were all really good hands terry was a hippie that decided he wanted to buckaroo and he had blond hair down below his shoulders and looked like genral custer and was one of the best cowboys I ever worked around any where andy was a great big guy middle aged and had a real problem with alchol the first day he was there he stayed in camp and shod some horses the next day when he caught the horse he was going to ride I was looking at his shoe job and he said does my horse shoeing suit you jigger boss I said I wasent looking at it to find something wrong with it I was looking at it to see if I could learn something from it after that conversation we got along real well Myron was about seventeen and had been buckarooing since he was fourteen he was a real good cowboy and a pleasure to work with now I was real green at running a crew and would call out a circle and if I was screwing up andy or terry would tell me after a while I got pretty good at figuring things out its been forty years and a long ways down the road and ive been the cowboy and the boss and even the owner sometimes but I have never forgot those guys and their kindness tword a green jigger boss

The Big Storm

many people don't realize that it wasent all sunshine and roses here well im here to tell you that while I enjoyed my life as a buckaroo it wasent all great by any means after we got the heifers put in rock springs pasture they spent the rest of the summer in the middle of September we gathered those heifers and were going to trail them to the grayson ranch gary the manager said we could make it to the bull head in one day and blane didn't think we could but gary pulled the maneger card and so we started from rocksprings at daylite and about eight oclock it started pouring rain and kept it up all day nobody had slickers so we just kept driveing tword the bullhead as it turned out blane was right and we couldent make it in a day and we got there about nine oclock that nite and put them in the field then had to drive all the way back to little owyhee camp all this time it rained in sheets it also was my twenty third birthday as we were leaving gary told us to take the next day off and rest and finish the drive the day after that was one trip and one birthday I never forgot

Green Salad

Lettuce or other greens
Onions
Tomatoes
Olive oil
Minced garlic
Vinegar (I use cider vinegar)

Chop lettuce and onions. Quarter tomatoes. Put in bowl and drizzle oil over it and add garlic. Toss to cover with oil and garlic. Splash vinegar on to taste. Keep tossing.

If you can get them clean, burlap wool sacks make great game bags. The air flows thru and the flies cant get in. They cover a whole lamb or deer real well.

Beans Basic Recipe

Ham, bacon or linguisa or ham hocks
Beans (anymore I use canned beans but packaged beans are fine)
1 large onion or 2 small
6 wax peppers, fresh or canned chilis or bell pepper, whatever you have
1 15 ounce can tomato sauce
Minced garlic to taste
Liquid smoke if you want just a splash

Combine everything in slow cooker. I drain beans and add water. Cook on low 8 hours.

If you use dry beans be sure to sort thru them for bad ones and rocks. They are also dirty so wash them then either soak them overnite or boil them for 1 hour. Drain and cook.

I usually use red beans. White beans are also real good.

Bean Soup

2 cans beans
1 can tomato sauce
2 carrots sliced
2 stalks celery sliced
1 medium onion
6 slices bacon or ham or linguisa
1 box beef broth
Mix together and simmer till vegetables are done

Going to the IL

after working for the circle a for six months it was time to come back to California and winter I was really wanting to go back to Nevada in the spring so when may came around I got on the phone and started calling about the third call I made I got a job on the IL ranch at Tuscarora I drove to elko and spent the night and went on out the next day I got there about noon and met tom the cowboss and he told me the rest of the crew were off for a couple of days and me and 2 other guys he hired would take care of some things around the ranch and shoe our horses up the next morning we went and moved some heifers and came home and we each shod 2 horses apiece this went on each day till we had all our horses shod do something in the mourning and shoe a couple horses in the afternoon the afternoon of the third day the crew came back and we met them there were tim jerry jr Robert and dave the horse wrangler was frank and the cook was dick we caught up the rest of the little jobs around headquarters and then pulled out for the desert ranch we had a chuck wagon pulled by four horses and behind that the bed wagon behind that ninety saddle horses and behind them 500 bulls for just a little while everything was in a line but the wagons and horses left us pretty quick them old bulls don't walk fast I sure would of liked to get a picture of that tho

Them Old IL Horses

when I worked for the il they had about 100 horses in the cavvy it was one of the best cavvies I ever saw in Nevada I saw more nice broke horses there than anywhere I ever worked tom the cowboss was a great horseman and truly an artist at takeing a horse with problems and getting them straitened out how ever there were a lot of horses there that were hard to shoe not bad not mean just hard didn't like there feet handled they also would buck I don't think I ever saw a single morning that you didn't see at least one bronk ride and sometimes three or four if you had time to watch and wernt going for a bronk ride yourself the first mourning we left for the desert a big tall horse named centerfire got dave twice centerfire was tall and hard to get on if dave could make it on him he could ride him every time I had a horse named little pinky in my string he was miserable to shoe and when ever you rode him every time you looked at his head he was watching you out of the corner of his eye one mourning I got off him to reset my saddle and when I got back on him he got his head down about halfway and was starting to buck me off I had to give him his head and spur him to get him to line out then he really tried me I looked down and all I saw was black rocks to land on so I really beared down and got him rode I rode him every seven days and you always sat up straight on him another horse I had was matt he was gentle but we were gathering some work horses one day and he ran away down off the side of a mountain with me didn't fall down or anything but it was a pretty scarey ride one morning when we were going to move camp first thing one of the work horses ran away with the harness on him right thru camp sounded like a freight train comeing he tore the harness up some so we were delayed about an hour fixing the harness dick our cook used to get out in front of his kitchen every mourning and lean on a shovel if a horse got headed for his kitchen he swatted him alongside the head and turned him never a dull moment there in the mornings

Me and Dave and the Propane

when I worked at the il we had a older man named dick that was the cook he was an interesting guy he had come to Nevada from Arizona when he was young and buckarooed all over the state also had went to austrailia he would tell you stories and cook at the same time he always had a bottle of jim beam on his chuck box and took a swig out of it now and then while he was cooking he also was a good teamster and drove the team on the chuck wagon it was a four horse team and 2 of them were gentle but the leaders doc and pinky wernt very gentle and wernt above running away while we were at the ranch getting ready to go to the desert dick was going to trim doc and pinkys manes up and he asked me and dave to fill up some propane bottles to go in the wagon to cook with they had a huge propane tank there that would hold a truck load of propane it had a long nossle on it and we were trying to figure out how to work it just as we got it to work dick led doc and pinky out of the barn and we blasted them with propane they jerked away from dick and ran down thru the horse corral and into the wrangle field and we had to send frank to wrangle the whole cavvy to catch them dick thought it was funny and wasent mad about it dick also made his own bread and I still remember trotting back into camp and you could smell that bread bakeing

Learning Not to Look at my Horn

when I worked for the il we branded open rodeer a lot just find a spot where there wasent much brush and bunch the cows and rope the calfs around the neck and drag them past a guy that they put close to the fire to heel everything jerry and an old indian named pete were the guys that heeled everything now growing up in California I learned to dally on rubber when I got started hanging around outside cowboys I got rid of the rubber on my horn it took along time to get used to dallying on a slick horn and I had enough trouble learning that ive never dallied on rubber since also I got the habit of looking at my horn when I dallied and I used to lose my rope at the il they saw what I was doing and told me to watch my critter I had caught not my horn I still had trouble with looking at my horn so the crew got together and told me if you look at your horn we are going to rock you im here to tell you if you get 4 guys throwing rocks at you somebody is going to hit you or your horse it didn't take long and I never looked at my horn anymore and I still don't thirty nine years later

The IL Wagon

when i worked at the il we stayed out with the wagon seven days a week and they brought out groceries to dick where ever we were camped we ate pretty basic there but it was good and we were working hard and also young and tough they butchered a dry cow every 2 weeks there for the ranch we would get a front quarter every 2 weeks now they killed that cow that morning and we got ours about noon so the next day you were eating her that meat had an indescribable taste to it till it aged for a few days but after that it was pretty good we hung it out at night and in the morning dick cut whatever he was going to cook that day and then wraped it up in a canvas and put it in the shade it kept real well that way and never spoiled we ate mostly fried steak or roast beef or stews i dont ever remember eating hamburger there dick also made his own bread both white bread and cinnamon bread it was always good also we ate breakfast at four oclock in the morning and left camp and you didnt eat again till you got back to camp useally about 2 oclock i sure remember troting back to camp and smelling what ever dick had cooking im sure glad i got to be part of that life

Circles On The IL

Previously i told you about getting started out of camp at the il this story is along the same lines we used to eat breakfast at four oclock in the morning there when i started there it was still cold in the mornings dicks cook tent had a wood stove in it and he would build a fire in it every morning and then at three thirty he let out this god awful squall and proceded to sing dirty songs at the top of his lungs to wake us up he had some great songs he knew we would get up and eat then catch horses and get saddled and mounted and leave camp on a trot and trot some times ten or twelve miles then tom would start dropping us off one at a time we would gather all the cows and calfs we could find and go tword a place where there wasnt to much brush when you start cattle like that you need to sneak around and try and make sure everything is paired up then start them and sit and watch a few minuts any thing that isnt paired up leave and get it the next day the reason for this is so you dont orphan calfs then you go to where your going to bunch every thing thats is called the rodeo grounds when you get there hopefuly you wont have more than fifty or seventy five calfs to brand if you have more than that the cows get hard to hold and keep there then while a couple guys hold the cows every one else starts packing brush to build a fire some times they would haul a branding pot and propane tank out there but useally only when we branded in a trap when you had enough age brush gathered they built a fire and got the irons hot usually two men worked on the ground and three men roped and three men held the cows every body changed off doing every thing except cutting the bull calfs the cowboss and jigger boss did that after you got every thing branded you trotted back to camp and had a meal and rested the rest of the day unless you needed to shoe a horse or maybe we might go in the pickup to where the next days rodeo grounds were going to be and gather sage brush for the next day

Vegetable Soup

1 onion
2 pounds beef cut in small pieces. Also can use hamburger.
2 cans diced tomatoes
1 package frozen mixed vegetables
1 box beef broth
Add together, simmer till vegetables are done.

When you go to a new ranch always show up with clean saddle blankets. It will make a huge difference in the kind of horses they give you to ride.

Hot Dog Burritos

1 flour tortilla, large is best
1 large spoonful of canned chili
Onion to taste
Spread chili on tortilla
Lay a hot dog on top
Add onions, fold and roll up. Heat in microwave. Wrap in tin foil, serve with Fritos. Makes a great lunch.

Peanut Butter and Jelly Burritos

1 flour tortilla
Peanut butter
Jelly
Spread peanut butter and jelly on tortilla, fold and roll.

Often times if you jump a buck and don't get a shot at him if you let him settle a few days he will be back again and you can try him again.

Getting a Job on the Big Ranches

tom and i went for a ride recently and looked around up on top and he asked me if when i was working on big ranches if there was much of a job interview when i was in that life you knew all the places that hired a crew and i always tried to pick ones where you just rode and ran a wagon first you listened around and tried to find out who might need someone then you started calling those places they would always ask where you worked before and if you could shoe a horse also i used to get asked alot if i had been out with a wagon before then they would ask you if you could ride a snaffle bit horse now this didnt mean some horse that they just rode in a snaffle bit altho there plenty of them on those ranches it meant some horse between three and six years with about ten rides on sometime in the last year answering that question you better be honest i used to tell them i wasnt a bronk rider but i got along with my horses at where ever i had been before then they would say come on out after you had been around a year or so there useally was someone there that you had worked with before the next thing i always did before i went out there was go to the car wash and wash my cinch and saddle blanket real good that was the best peice of advice i ever got show up with a clean cinch and saddle blankets when you got there everyone on the crew just kind of watched you for a day or two the first horse they caught you was useally pretty gentle and the next one they caught was useally a pretty broke horse the third one you better watch because he might be pretty green some cowbosses tried to fit you with a string that fit you some bosses just said you hired on here you get what i catch for you the next thing you had to shoe your horses as you rode them shoe the next days horse after work or shoe the one you rode that day after work after you got to know your horses when the wrangle boy brought the horses into the rope corrall you had your halter and as soon as the cowboss steped in the ropes you said what horse you wanted dont make him ask you when he caught it you walked up and put your halter on and took the bosses rope off and handed it to him then went back and dont leave the ropes till everyone has a horse sometimes if youve got a cranky horse the boss might tell you go ahead and saddle him and lead him around some when everyone is saddled up you get mounted and leave camp stay behind the cowboss and let him lead just a few memories of when i was in that life

Cooks

when jerry and i went to the gamble ranch they had a man named bob cooking for the wagon and a guy named charlie cooking at the ranch bob was a chef and had became an alcholic and couldent hold a job in town so he cooked on ranches at one time or another he worked for all of them he was a great guy most of the time but he could get pretty cranky when he got thirsty after you let him go on about a four day bender he was pretty good for another month the gamble ranch fed real good and would get bob any groceries he wanted within reason so we got alot of home made pies and cinniman rolls also doughnuts sometimes he also made chicken pot pies when ever we shot him some sagehens i always liked to cook so i learned alot from bob but what amazed me was when ever we rode into camp he had a meal ready and it was always outstanding he had been all over the country rideing freight trains and could tell you what skid row was like in almost any town you could mention he had also done alot of other jobs other than cook truely an interesting guy after i quit going to nevada to work i went to the ts to visit a friend and bob was cooking in the cookhouse there i went down one afternoon and visited with him for about an hour it was the last time i saw bob but i still remember his cooking

Men on those Ranches

the other night I wrote a story about our cook and what he did on payday
when I was working there were all kinds of older men and they were
cooks, irrigators and buckaroos those ranches knew to the second how
long it was going to take those guys to get broke in town then they went
in and asked them if they were ready to come back and go to work they
useally did and would stay anywhere from thirty days to ninety days
some would even make it for six months but they always ended up going
to town and getting drunk and going broke some of those old guys had
come to Nevada when they were kids and never made it back home yet
there were also a few old guys around town that were retired and they
gathered in the commercial coffee shop every morning and drank coffee
and visited one forth of july we were in town and dave bought a set of
twenty eight inch tapederos and we were carrying them down the side
walk to put in my pickup we saw this old guy and didn't think much of it
the next morning we went in the commercial for breakfast and that same
old guy was in there with some other old men he said I saw you boys
carrying a set of tapaderos yesterday when I was young I used taps like
that where are you guys working we said the il he said I worked there
when I was a young fellow I asked what year was that he said 1919 we
just sat there and talked to that old man for about an hour never have
forgot that visit

Cajun Rice

3 chicken breast cut up
1 pound kielbasa
1 pound frozen shrimp
2 bell peppers
2 ½ onions
Minced garlic
2 cups celery
4 cans diced tomatoes
1 can diced chilis
1 can tomato sauce
2 cups uncooked brown rice
2 12 ounce cans chicken broth

Cube chicken breast and cook in 12 inch Dutch oven. Put sausage and shrimp in and add rest of ingredients. Put in preheated oven at 350 2 to 3 hours.

If you want to practice in the Dutch oven in the oven in the house, 350 degrees is the temperature that's what most of recipes are.

Dutch Oven London Broil with Spanish Rice

1 london broil, 2.5 pounds
1 onion
2 peppers, sweet wax or can use bell
2 celery stalks
Minced garlic to taste
1 can beef broth
1 8 ounce canned tomato sauce
1 can diced tomatoes
1 cup uncooked brown rice

Put rice, onion, celery and peppers, tomato sauce and tomatoes in bottom of Dutch oven, beef broth over it. Bring to a boil, put a rack in Dutch oven and meat on top of rack. Season meat to taste and put lid on Dutch oven. Put in preheated oven, 350 degrees for 1 hour 15 minutes.

You never realize till after you leave home what a good cook your mom was.

Jim and Badger at the 1993 Snaffle Bit Futurity Reno, NV

Jerry and I go to the Gamble

after six weeks of branding on the il wagon we pulled into headquarters and went to town for fourth of july while we were in town we heard the gamble ranch was paying six hundred a month compared to four seventy five a month at the il so jerry and I rolled our beds and went to the gamble the cowboss had quit and a new one was on the way the new cowboss was merv and everyone knew him as he had ran squaw valley wagon for a few years in the mean time there was a guy named keith leading off there were also john and tim tim had come down from Canada and hadent shod very many horses so I helped him shoe his horses it began a friendship that still goes on today tim became a buckaroo and later a cowboss the ranch was way behind branding so we branded calfs every day and keith cut me a bunch of colts to ride about august first merv showed up and we all liked him a lot we started pushing cows to the mountains and did that all of august also there were ross and jerry down at the winecup and they hired a kid named joe to wrangle horses our cook was bob he had been a chef in highclass reaturants til he became to much of an alcholic to keep a job he made it fine out in camp tho and was a great cook that was one of the best summers and falls I ever worked

Big Earl

someone recently told me about rideing a horse that loped in place it reminded of in 1981 myself and a friend named jerry went to work on the gamble ranch the gamble ran a wagon that went out in may and came back in November we got hired about the end of july they were way behind in spring branding and were still branding everyday the first day they caught me this big appy horse named big earl now earl turned out to be a real nice horse and sure tried hard to do a good job also he was real

91

gentle and while he wasent an outstanding athlete he was just pretty good at any thing when we got there the wagon was camped at a place called rock springs after we got that country branded up we moved camp to crittonden reservoir john and I trailed the saddle horses in that country they call it the cavvy from rock springs to our new camp the rest of my string of horses were all colts and pretty green so I rode earl for the move I didn't know where we were going so john led off and I brought the cavvy behind him old earl loped in place and sideways all the way from rock springs to crittonden about twenty miles man that was a long day for me and I was completely worn out by the time we got there

The Bay C Punch Horse at the Gamble

when jerry and I went to the gamble ranch they were right in the middle of expanding and were buying quite a few new horses the gamble ranch manager had a pretty good set of brood mares and a stud and took a lot of pride in raiseing good horses most of the gamble cavvy that had been there awhile were pretty gentle as far as big outfit horses go how ever some of the boughten horses were not as gentle one day merv hauled a gooseneck load of horses out to camp and said these are new horses we need to try them out every body got one or two of them I got a marvel horse and a c punch horse the marvel horse was a three year old and he was a nice horse later he ended up in the cowboss string after I left the other horse was a big blood bay and was only shod in front I figured he might be hard to shoe behind but he wasent bad he was a good horse and handled well but he was a cranky bastard I didn't let him buck and got by him pretty good he did buck with me twice but I got him rode both times and he was getting better when I left the next year I came back and he had got bad enough to buck he was in the rough string but randy got along with him after randy quit rideing him he got sold to a rodeo company and the first summer nobody rode him I heard I always felt bad because I think if he hadn't got started bucking people off he might of been a good one

That Old High Stepping Kind

i was watching some cowboy poetry recently and i watched a sunny hancock poem called that old high stepping kind about a kid that went to work on a ranch and ran his mouth to much when i worked on the big ranches they always had eight or ten horses in the cavvy just for someone who ran his mouth or didnt treat his horses right those old horses would sure make a guy wish he hadent done so much bragging or hadent been so hard on the horses he got in his string to begin with altho once in awhile somebody would come along that could ride everyone of those horses one story i heard and i dont know if it was true or not was about a young guy that showed up at the spanish ranch and when bill kane asked him what kind of horse he could ride the guy said his saddle fit all of them bill gave him every cranky horse he had and the guy rode all of them pretty impressive if you knew the spanish ranch cavvy then i always wanted to work at the spanish ranch but never went there

The Rhinoceros Headed Bay

ive told you about one of the trailer loads of horses we got at the gamble ranch this story is about some more horses after august we went to town for labor day and then came back to start fall works merv hauled another gooseneck load of horses out for us when we un loaded them there was a homely little bay horse in them he had a fresh brand on and merve said that is my sons brand and one of you younger guys can try that rhinoceros headed son of a bitch out I don't know what hole he has in him but there sure is one somewhere they had hired 2 new guys over labor day bruce and john both were good cowboys and john got the little bay when he steped on him he bucked like a scalded hound but john got him rode after that he was fine and really handled well but everytime you rode him you were in for a bronk ride bruce got a horse named honkytonk that was hard to shoe but pretty good other wise merv split the crew and half gathered cattle into crittonden resovior and the other half trailed them to eighteen mile everyday bruce and john and jerry and myself useally trailed cows to eighteen mile every day but we had a lot of fun ropeing everything all the way down there and then trot back and do it again the next day the weather stayed nice all fall and after we got done up there we moved camp to eighteen mile and started getting ready to wean calfs when they got caught up with the work it was time to come back to California for the winter.

Fast Egg Sandwiches

6 eggs
Onion, diced
Sweet pickle relish if you have it
Mustard
Mayonnaise

Crack eggs in frying pan and fry till hard. Break the yolks. Get them well done and put in a bowl with a fork. Mix and mash them, add diced onion, pickle relish, mustard and mayonnaise to taste. Also, salt and pepper.

The biggest gift you can give an older person is your time.

Randy

after another winter in California it was time to go back to Nevada so I called the gamble ranch merv and every one else except john had moved on and john was the cowboss he called me back the next night and told me to come on up when I got there the wagon was camped at johns house and his wife was cooking because bob our cook was off on a bender the first afternoon I met the crew there was kirk randy ted and ben kirk and ben would leave before long the first mourning randy who also rode rough string got on this big palomino horse named soda and he bucked right straight thru a six wire fence with him it cut him a little but not bad so randy caught a black horse named benny binyon and went for a hell of a bronk ride after that we trotted over to a seeding and were gathering it I saw randy off his horse so I rode over to see if anything was wrong he had a forked stick about 18 inches long and was chaseing a rattlesnake around with it by now im beginning to wonder about randy and I said you do relize that's a rattle snake he just looked at me and said what are you worried about he not a very big one pretty soon he pined his head down and stood on it and took his knife out and cut the snakes head off then he skinned it and stuck it on his cantle then he explained that if you kill them that way you don't ruin the hide randy and I became real good friends after that it was just kind of an unuseal way to meet

Riding Gary Takas

the second time I worked at the gamble they had a lot wilder crew and john liked to see bronk rides so every mourning you could see someone go for a bronk ride john had given me a string of mostly young horses and some older horses he wanted someone to take care of and not use to hard I was raised to talk those horses out of bucking if you could because the object of any ranch is to make money and having a whole cavvy that

96

bucks isn't the way to do that well any way I was keeping my horses from bucking and getting quite a bit of flack for it right before forth of july this photographer came out to the wagon with us and john wanted everyone to make sure he got lots of pictures we all went to town one night and got drunk and john talked me into rideing a horse they called gary takacs after I sobered up I was pretty worried and randy told me I saw kirk ride him a bunch of times just hobble your sturrips and you can ride him easy the big mourning arrived and I saddled old gary we were camped in a meadow so it was a pretty good place I steped on him and he didn't want to untrack and move off so I spured him and he really came apart he bucked down thru camp the rope corrall was there and the rest of the cavvy was in it we circled the ropes and joe the wrangle boy was staying between me and the ropes keeping us out of there I got ahead of him and he went back around the ropes and turned us right into them gary jumped in the ropes and bucked right across the corrall when we got to the other side all I could do was give him his head and spur him and he jumped out of them and I got him stoped I was really mad at myself for being in this mess when john yelled don't hold one of my horse up I looked and john and the photogrefer were standing about seventy five feet from me so I aimed gary at them and gave him his head and spured him he bucked right straight at them and they had to run to get out of the way later we all laughed about this but I didn't hear don't hold my horses up again that mourning

Little Buck Yard Darts Me

after the photogrefer left we went to town for forth of july john said we needed 2 more guys if you see anyone looking for a job I was sitting at the front bar in the commercial one afternoon and this young guy came up to me and told me him and another guy just came down from the padlock wagon and were looking for a job I told him what john looked like and where he might find him and sure enough john hired them both there names were troy and gary they were both good guys and good help after we got back to the ranch we had some calfs to brand and then move camp we gathered the cows and calfs and when we got to camp john said I need some new latigoes we will all go to town and get them now I knew better than to go but I went any way and one thing led to another and we didn't get back to camp till 3 oclock the next mourning so we just drank coffee till bob had breakfast ready and caught horses and went to brand calfs I was rideing an older horse named little buck he was a good horse but kind of lazy so being hungover and tired I was pecking at him some right at the last calf he got mad and just yard darted me over his right shoulder and I lit on my back and knocked the wind out of me frank an older man said what an awful way to end a day like today john said after that you better ride back to camp in the pickup and someone can lead your horse home I sure appreaciated the pickup ride and learned don't peck on them old lazy horses they have feelings

Moving Cows over Delano Mountain

after the branding where I got yard darted we moved camp to crittonden resovior john sent me and troy and gary with the cavvy and all of us got well aqainted because all you had to do was stay in front of the cavvy going tword the gamble ranch if they ever got past you they pulled out for twelve mile swamp where they wintered we made it to crittondon and turned the cavvy in the field there and helped set up camp the next day we started moveing cows to the mountains one day we took about six hundred pair over Delano mountain to turn loose in rock springs we had trouble getting started so randy and I got a bunch of leaders started and the rest followed every one behind left the drag alone and let them string out when we got over the top of Delano mountain randy and I stoped the leaders there were cows strung out one behind the other clear up that mountain and the drag was just comeing over the top I sure wished Ida had a camera that day after that we just moved cows to the mountains every day for a while troy and gary turned out to be good help and great guys also I lost track of gary after he left there but troy and I have remaned friends all these years

Apricot Cobbler

12 inch Dutch oven

1 can 7 up
1 yellow cake mix, the cheapest one. You can get NOT extra moist.
4 28 ounce cans apricots drained
Cinnamon to taste
I put just a sprinkle of cloves. Just a tiny bit its easy to get too much.

Put fruit, cinnamon and cloves in Dutch oven. Pour cake mix over the top. Smooth out with spoon. Pour 7 up over the cake mix pushing it around with the back of the spoon till its covered. Bake at 350 1 hr. Take it out and let cool.

You an use any kind of fruit and any kind of soda.

In camp, always keep the horse shoe nails in a dry place. They get a lot harder to drive if they get rusty.

Canned Biscuit Cobbler

10 inch Dutch oven

1 can biscuits
3 cans fruit, drained. I use cherry pie filling
Cinnamon to taste

Put fruit in Dutch oven. Open biscuits, separate and slightly wet them. Like, just pass them under the sink faucet. Mix cinnamon and sugar and coat both sides of them. Lay them on top of the fruit and bake till they are done.

How to season or reseason a cast iron pan or Dutch oven. Wash them out with hot water if they have rust, take a wire brush or sand paper and get it out. Get dry and put a light coat of oil on them all over. Just a light coat is you see it collecting at all its too much. Preheat oven to 400 degrees. Set pans or Dutch oven in and hot cook 1 hour. Turn oven off and let everything cool in the oven.

Camped at Sign Board Well

while we were camped at signboard well we had some terrific thunder storms you would be in bed and hear them comeing and we would all get up and sit in the pickup and watch them you couldent sleep they came right thru there altho nothing ever got struck at our camp we would watch the saint elmos fire jump from one tipi pole to another it was pretty neat to see one morning we caught horses and john caught gary an ingnorent brown horse they called battling tom and caught troy a horse called rojo and ted called for a horse named cowboy when we got mounted all three of them started bucking ted got bucked off and gary got tom rode and troy rode rojo for a long ways before he got bucked off then we spent about forty five minutes catching cowboy and rojo another mourning randy was trying a new horse out and we all had our tipis set along the fence that horse bucked right between the fence and our tipis randy kept rideing that horse and he got to be a good one just one morning at sign board well

The Wreck at SignBoard Well

after we got all the cows moved from around crittondon we moved camp to signboard well it was right on top of a hill and open all around we had a huge wrangle field and put bells on several of the cavvy one mourning we caught horses and everybody had a horse randy had caught a horse called soldier blue and instead of putting a halter on him he just made a halter with his lass rope now soldier blue was kind of an ignorant sort so he pulled back and got away dragging randys rope he made two circles thru where we were saddling up and every one else except me and troys horses got away then he jumped in the rope corrall and the cavvy tore it down and got out and ran off with soldier blue chaseing them by then troy and I were saddled up and we took off after the cavvy they outran us for a long ways but we cut across and got them stoped on the back side of this butte and held them up for about an hour till they calmed down troy was able to sneak up and grab randys rope and we turned soldier blue loose and drove the cavvy back to camp when we got there john and randy and gary had every thing fixed john said its to late to do anything today why don't we rest the rest of the day we didn't get anything done that day but it sure was an exciting morning

Getting Bob Out of Town

while we were still camped at signboard well we got paid bobs money was burning a hole in his pocket and he was getting cranky so john let us have 3 days off and go to town and he stayed and watched camp he told me its your job to make sure you get bob out of town and back here I said how does one go about that john said its pretty easy just drop him off at the overland and go in and have one drink with him when you come back in 2 days he will be on the same stool also buy a bottle of cheap wine but don't let him see it if he gets to sick when we get him back out here I will give it to him and stop in Montello and let him have a few in the bar there on the way home so off we go to town and droped bob off at the overland and went on to elko after two days we headed back to the ranch and stoped to get bob we went in the bar and he wasent there so I asked the bartender if she knew where he was she said that little loud mouthed son of a bitch is still in bed you might have to help him out because he got pretty full last night she gave us his room number and we went up there and he was so sick he couldent get out of bed we got him up and dressed and in the pickup and I bought him a sixpack of beer and took off for Montello and let him have about 5 highballs in the bar then took him back out to camp he was pretty sick for a couple days but we knew he would be good for the rest of the fall

The Watermelon at 18 Mile

when we moved from signboard well we moved camp to twelve mile
where john lived the we went to town for labor day gary had went back
to texas to start collage but troy was still there after a couple days in
town I decided to go back to the ranch and troy decided to go also we
were hanging around camp and jim fretwell the manager came down and
said there were a lot of cows at crittonden and he wanted us to move
them to eighteen mile he wrangled the horses they kept at the ranch and
caught troy a little roan horse he called applesauce and caught me a grey
horse named spider they were both nice horses he told us to start at
daylite the next morning and he would catch up to us troy and I got up to
crittonden the next morning and there was probly about five hundred
cows there more than anyone thought so we started them tword
eighteen mile I had the lead and troy had the drag but they traveled good
and pretty soon jim showed up it was still a long hot drive to eighteen
mile there at eighteen mile they had a great big water trough and the
water was ice cold some people had been camping and the left a
watermelon in that cold water and didn't eat it jim saw it and got a stick
and got it out before the cows got there so we all ate that cold
watermelon I never have forgot how good that was after driveing those
cows down there

Slim the Horse

after we got back from town and recovered we moved camp down to the
wine cup and started gathering down there things were going along
pretty well then we got a fall snow storm and that put us behind a bit
after things dried out enough to move camp we moved to the winecup
head quarters it was still wet and cold while we were there troy rolled up
and left so we were also shorthanded one day randy came to me and said

I have 2 horses I would like you to take they don't buck anymore and are scared of me and they need someone to just leave them alone and get along with them one horse was named slim and he was a gaited horse did all sorts of neat gaits but he had been spoiled the first mourning I rode him he didn't want to leave home and was trying to run back to the barn I had a pair of twenty eight inch taps on my saddle and I swung them under his belly to get him to move out I got lucky and they slaped together and sounded like a shot gun going off old slim jumped straight in the air and shot a turd about eight feet behind him and was never barn sour after that he went on to be a nice horse and would really watch a cow ive never ridden another gaited horse since but I sure never forgot old slim

Canned Biscuit Hand Pies

1 tube canned biscuits
Fruit for filling

Open biscuits and separate roll out.
Then, put fruit inside, fold over, seal edges with the tines of a fork. Put on a baking pan and bake until done. You can also fry these.
You can add cinnamon to the fruit and sugar and cinnamon sprinkled on after they are done.

Time and years really go by a lot faster than you think they would.

Laurie Johnson's Gravy

Drippings from whatever you cooked
Flour
Water
Mix flour and water, stir till theres no lumps. Add to drippings.
Simmer till it thickens.

When I first moved to my own house I would fix a big dinner if I needed advice. I would call my mom. However, this one Sunday Mom wasn't home I had roasted a whole chicken. So I called Laurie Johnson and she told me how to make this gravy.

Skillet Apple Pie

Canned biscuits
1 21 ounce can apple pie filling
1 stick butter melted
½ cup brown sugar
 1 tsp cinnamon
1 tsp vanilla extract

Glaze
Powdered sugar
2 or 3 tsp milk

Mix sugar and cinnamon
Dip each biscuit in butter
Roll in sugar cinnamon miture
Brush sides and bottom of skillet.
Cut apples into smaller pieces
Add vanilla extract and pour over biscuits. Pour leftover butter and sprinkle leftover cinnamon sugar mix over top.
Bake 30-35 minutes until golden and puffy at 375 degrees.
Make Glaze and drizzle over top

Theres no such thing as the perfect dog, horse, person or relationship.
You have to settle for the one that has the faults you can live with.

Fall Work

i always liked fall work on the big ranches if you were lucky and it stayed warm and didnt storm until you got back into the ranch in my case i left the first of october or the middle of october but the weather was cooler and you were gathering and pairing up alot of cows also branding some late calfs i always rode some colts on those ranches and by fall they were comeing along nicely however if you had a cold wet fall things wernt so much fun the last fall i worked for the gamble ranch was cold and wet and snow and just about every unpleasent thing you could think of we got a snow storm when we were camped in loomis basin and couldent get camp moved out of there till after it dried out in the meantime we trailed about fifteen hundred cows out of there we had to cross the highway at the winecup gate i was on one side and randy was on the other side the cows were strung out for a long ways and when ever we got six or seven cars lined up we stoped the cows and let them thru we got our pictures taken alot that day then we moved camp to the wine cup and preg tested all those cows it spit rain and snow the whole time we did that then it cleared up for a few days and we branded some calfs and moved to crittonden reservior about two days later i woke up one morning and the wind was howling and the snow was blowing crossways and i thought its time to go back to california so i rolled my bed and gathered up my saddle and other things i went down to the wagon for breakfast and i didnt get a chance to tell john i was leaveing so will brought the horses into the ropes and john was catching horses for everyone i never called for a horse he looked at me and said what do you want meaning what horse did i want i said a ride to the ranch he said well i knew that was comeing so he took me down to head quarters i helped him do a couple things there and he followed me into montello and bought me lunch i told him i would be back the next spring but life goes on and i never made it back

How To Trail Cows

when i grew up we trailed cattle alot so i grew up knowing to leave the drag alone and just follow them and dont let them spread out a bunch of cows string out from the center both ways they are just like people some walk faster than others if you pound the drag and try and drive them over the leaders they just spread out as they dont have room to follow each other the fellows on each side should be back and forth along the side and keep things tucked back in line all of this should be done easy and smoothly your herd will stay mothered up this way and move out if everyone works together they should travel along good and be mothered up when you get where you are going where you really learn about this is on the desert when you ride from camp and trail a bunch of cows somewhere and then have to trot back to camp if your cows are mothered up because you did a good job of trailing them you dont have to hold them as long before you get started on that trot back to camp that could be some where between 10 and 20 miles just one of the things in the life the way it used to be

First Days On The IL

its been awhile since i wrote anything about working for the il when i got there in may the wagon had been out about 2 weeks and was back in at headquarters me and 2 other guys arrived there at the same time we did some small jobs around the head quarters and shod all our horses we each got seven head mine were matt buck goober buster spinner pumpkin and little pinky all of them except little pinky i liked but goober buster and little pinky were hard to shoe buck was really cold backed and so was buster goober also little pinky just watched you out of the corner of his eye all the time and waited for you to not be paying attention then he would get you if he could the rest of them were fine tho and i got buy those four ok also when we were camped out we had a horse drawn chuck wagon and a big canvas tent that we ate in the rope corrall was close by and our tepees were set up around there also every morning frank brought the horses into the ropes and tom and tim roped all the horses as we called for them then when everyone had a horse they let the horses out of the rope corrall and frank took them out to graze for the day then at night we put them in the wrangle field everyone got saddled up and about the time we were ready to mount up dick would come out of his cook tent with his shovel and stand there if a horse got to bucking tword his kitchen he whacked him alongside the head and turned him away from the kitchen some mornings you could see three or four bronc rides if you wernt going for a bronc ride yourself then tom would hit a trot and we would all fall in behind him and tim another day with the il wagon had begun

Harold and Carroll and Pat and Marie

in 1983 I went to work for a ranch down here thru branding and shipping this ranch was owened by two brothers who married two sisters and all lived in the same house the brothers were harold and carrol and the sisters were pat and marie these guys sure ran a good outfit and they had started with nothing and it was one of the best places I ever worked well to get back to my story carrol and I were shipping cows out of between Lincoln and Roseville its all houses now at lunch we would set in the shade of the scale box at the corrals and carrol would tell me about being raised around there they had grown up in rocklin one day he told me when I was a kid he was 72 then this was the whitney ranch it was 22000 acres and the whitney kids were pretty rough so they couldent go to the dances anywhere around so the whitney family built there own dance hall out here and had dances out here those dances sure had a lot of fights at them I used to like to fight and could knock a guy out with either hand so I came out here a lot one time I came to nine dances and had thirteen fights and knocked every one of them out I really liked and respected carrol anyway but after that story I respected him a whole lot more

Clover Valley and the Sherriff

after we got the winecup gathered we moved to crittindon reservoir and started gathering we got kind of caught up so I pulled out and came back to California I was getting a lot of pressure from my parents to stop drifting and amount to something there words not mine the next spring I worked for some local ranchers they were two brothers who married two sisters and they all lived in the same house for the better part of fifty years they started with nothing and built it into a real good out fit I don't think I ever worked at a place I enjoyed so much the cows were wild but easy to handle they didn't care how much you roped and they encouraged you to ride young horses they just needed me thru branding and shipping so after that my parents talked me into going to shoeing school while I was there they pumped you up about how much money you could make and what a great career it was when I got back to California I started shoeing horses and kept at it for 3 years but it didn't work out for me I had no people skills and was bad to drink on top of it so I heard of a job up in clover valley for some rich people takeing care of some cows and took that there was a bar not far from my camp and I used to go there quite a bit the road between my camp and this bar was dirt and really dusty one night I left that place and a cop got after me I knew if I was lucky could go fast down that dirt road and he would have to slow down so I gassed it and it worked like I thought and I beat him to my camp and hid from him but I was smart enough to know the next time I wasent going to be as lucky so I went to a local big out fit and asked for a job they didn't need anyone but one of the cowboys there told me of a guy in likely that needed someone the guy was a friend of mine so I called him up and he said I need somebody to start some colts and I also need a camp man I asked where this camp was and he asked me what I had done so I told him he said its out at red rock lake and nobody is going to find you out there tomorrow life at red rock lake

Red Rock Lake

Ive told you the events that led to getting the camp job at red rock lake so I got up there and went to the ranch and spent the night the next morning they gave me a map and a bunch of groceries and sent me out to camp john and Raoul were already out there so I took off I drove and drove and drove finely I saw some guys horse back and stopped and asked them if I was going the right way they told me I was on the right road I just had quite a ways to go yet finely I came in sight of red rock lake and john and raul were driveing a bunch of cows down the road so I went on up to camp and unloaded my horses and the groceries they came in and we had supper and john told me he was going back to the ranch in 2 days and he wanted me to finish gathering and reride around red rock lake raul was going to stay there with me and irrigate the meadows also on the weekends I was supposed to come to the ranch and ride thru all the cattle on the meadows and get our groceries the first day after john left I was driving a bunch of cows down the road and this green pickup came down the road I wasent paying any attention and this guy said to me don't you ever stay home he was married to my cousin and I had seen him at an easter party and he was working on a ranch but he had gotten a job being the federal trapper in modoc county the next thing we had to work thru is raul didn't speak any English and I didn't speak Spanish so when I went to get the groceries we had problems I knew we needed meat and onions and potatoes but the canned goods had us baffeled so I kept one empty can of every thing we used and I would get the cans out and raul would tell me how many of each to get that worked real well after about two weeks john came out for a few days and helped us doctor some pinkeye and move some cows around we were driving these cows along and john said see raul talking to himself hes going to say something in English hes practicing that night at supper rual said hey john pass me the f---king water john had to tell him not to say that in the cookhouse at the ranch but it sure was funny out in camp

Johns Pack Mare

after I got things rerode around red rock lake john had me start packing salt he told me there is a bay mare up there shes a good pack horse and you can also ride her if you get short of horses the first day I packed her I tied her up to the fence and loaded 200 pounds of salt on her and she bucked it off before I could get it tied down so I tied her to the top of the post where she couldent get her head down at all and loaded the salt again and got it tied down she was mad as a hornet so I got on my horse and crowded her right up against the fence and untied her and snubbed her before she knew she was untied then I took off on a trot after about a mile she setteled down and was a great pack horse but every time you packed her you had to go thru this ritual later on I called a guy at a pack station looking for a job and he asked me what I had packed I said I packed salt for john at red rock lake all summer he said what did john have you packing I said a little bay mare he said if you packed that bitch all summer and are still alive to tell me about it you are alright but that's another story

I Get Hurt at the MC

after working for john all the rest of the summer I came home in the fall and ran a bunch of yearlings for my self unfortunately they had the dairy cow kill off and I barely broke even and lost a winters work so much for being in business and amounting to some thing that fall I had a rental house and it was vacant a woman that I had known quite a while rented it and we started dateing and eventualy got married but im getting ahead of my story so in the spring I went to battle mountain to the ts how ever I didnt stay very long I went to the mc in Oregon and the first morning there I got bucked off and pulled the ligaments in my right shoulder tore my rotater cuff on my left arm and split my sternam I didn't know what all was wrong with me but after a week I knew something was wrong so I came home and went to the doctor stephanie and I got real serious after I got home I guess I was not wanting to roam around so much and I was hurt bad enough I couldent go to work anywhere so we just spent a lot of time together by the next summer we had decided to get married but first I needed to address my drinking problem I got some help and got sober and we got married in September of 1988 we have been married and I have been sober for 32 years and I hope we have another thirty two years together

Sour Dough Starter

3 ¼ ounce packet yeast
3 cups warm water
2 Tablespoons sugar
3 cups flour. I used whole wheat.
1 raw potato peeled and quartered

Dissolve yeast in warm water. Add sugar, flour and potato. Mix in glass bowl with plastic or wooden spoon. Never anything metal. After a day or so you will see bubbles in the starter. Always if you take some out, replace with that much flour and warm water. Change potatoes every couple of weeks.

Sour Dough Hot Cakes

2 cups starter
2 cups flour
Water to thin it.
¼ teaspoon salt
½ teaspoon baking soda
½ teaspoon baking powder
1 teaspoon vanilla extract

Mix together and cook.

Camp Syrup

1 cup brown sugar
1 cup sugar
2 cups water
Vanilla extract or maple flavoring

In small sauce pan bring sugars and water to a boil. Stir and cook 2 minutes.
Add maple or vanilla extract.
You can use any kind of sugar
You can cook it till it thickens.

The Trip Hobbles

today my friend tom came out and we went for a ride and got to talking about hobble breaking horses when you start them during the conversation he asked me if i had ever used a running w i told him i had this is that story when i was at frank and howards we had one horse that was bad to buck with the saddle and he wasent quiting it either so frank told us to run him thru the trip bobbles thats another name for a running w now trip hobbles are a collar and ring on each front foot and a ring on your cinch you tie a rope in the ring on the cinch and bring it down and thru the ring on his foot and back up thru the ring on the cinch then down thru the ring on the other foot and back up thru the ring on the cinch it looks a w and you sure can take ones front feet away with one frank and howard were experts with one and could take a horses feet away without ever throwing him so we saddled this horse up and howard took his feet when he started to buck and he went off and behaved himself pretty good the next day i was working that horse and frank was watching me and that horse broke in two and i jerked on the trip hobbles and he came down right on his forhead frank calmly said jim maybe the next time dont pull so hard on those hobbles but after that if that horse tryed to buck and you hollered at him he thru his head up and froze until you moved him again

Shoeing My Own Horses

later this morning im going to shoe my other horse i did one last week one of the benefits of old age is you can shoe one a week or even two feet per day until you get them shod it made me think of when i started out shoeing pop always shod our horses when i was growing up and i helped him i started out handing him the tools as he needed them so i learned what each tool was for and how to use them then i started pulling shoes and later clinching and finishing but i never shaped any shoes or nailed any on i got a job in oregon and so he showed me how to level the foot and shape the shoes and nail them on and off i went to oregon when i got up there it was a smaller ranch and as soon as they found out i could shoe a horse they told me to keep all the horses shod so i flew at them those first shoe jobs were terrible i was pretty proud of them but they wernt very good i remember one horse i put shoes on that was hard to saddle and when i went to saddle him the next day he pulled both front shoes off i just kept picking them shoes up and nailing them back on until they stayed on as i shod more horses i got better at it and became a good cowboy shoer then i went to horseshoeing school and shod alot of horses after that i guess what im trying to say is if theres any young guys that want to learn to shoe dont be afraid to just get in there and give it a try most guys that can shoe well will help anyone that wants to learn

The Palimino Colt

after stephanie and i got married i shod horses and ran the family ranch and bought and sold horses i would buy colts and start them and resell them this one day we saw a colt advertised in the paper and went to look at him i didnt like him but there was a real nice palimino colt in a pen there i asked if he was for sale the lady said yes she would sell him for 800 dollars he was a stud colt so i tried to talk her down because i had to get him cut she said her vet cut them for less than mine so i said if you get him cut i will give you full price she agreed and i owned the colt i asked her if the mother was there she said yes shes that big stout mare with that mule colt there in that field next to the driveway now at that time i was green at horse buying and it never occured to me if this mares colts are good why are they raiseing mules out of her now thirty years later it would be a major red flag but i didnt even think of that then any way i got this colt home and proceded to start him his name was billy and he was easy to hobble and saddle i untied the hobbles and led him out of them and he made about one lap around the round corrall and just came undone my god could he buck im watching this and thinking what did i buy and get myself into this time well i kept after him every night after work and pretty soon he quit bucking with the saddle so he was ready to ride the first three rides he really had his hammer cocked but i got by him without him bucking after that he was fine but you sure treated him with alot of respect he was one of the most determined horses i ever rode and there was no way he was going to let a cow get away from him after i rode hime about two years i sold him and he went thru red bluff gelding sale and went to the east coast somewhere the next year i was at a horse show and ran across the guy that owned the stud he was out of this guy was an old man that had been a horseman and trainer for alot of years and won all kinds of cowhorse shows i said i had a colt out of your stud he said where did you get him i said from a lady in loomis named paula he said was it out of a big palimino mare i said yes he said kid you must be all right they never got that mare broke and a lot of guys tried her i owed that woman a favor and bred that mare for her and told her dont bring that colt to me to start i told him about billie and how he turned out he told me again that i must be alright but after that if i go look at a colt and they are raiseing mules out of the mother

The Pretty Bay Gelding

everyone that ever bought and sold horses knows sometimes you buy one that dosent work out this story is about one of those my dad was a cow trader and went to the local sale every week and bought cattle so one day the guy that owned the sale yard told my dad that he bought us a horse that came thru there he said he is six years old and sound take him home and try him for a couple weeks and if he dosent work out bring him back we went down and picked him up and boy was he pretty solid bay and really stout well mannered on the ground i couldent wait to try him i got him home and saddled him up the next day and he did fine i thought to myself this is going just to well so i tied him up in the sun for a few hours and the led him to the water trough and let him drink all he wanted then took him down to the round corrall and got on him he went off a few steps and then ran off with me in the round corrall my round corrall was made of panels and eight sided so i stuck his head in one of those corners and doubled him from that point on it was just a game of wits with him he tried every counterfit thing he knew and i tried to stay ahead of him he was hard to get on hard to get off really wanted to buck and also would run off if he got a chance he never did any of these things unless he thought he had an advantage we were gathering so i thought some long rides might solve things so i shod him supriseingly he was easy to shoe but the rides didnt do him any good you just had to sit straight up on him all day so after 2 weeks we took him back and they ran him thru the monthly horse sale harry said these guys been gathering cows on this horse and need lots of horses and brought him back here so you figgure it out about what hes like one of the horse traders bought him and about a month later came up to us and said that bay horse bucked all my guys off and is a sorry bastard my dad told him you should of knowen he wasent any good if we brought him back and sold him here thats the story of one that didnt work out

The Three Colts

while i was buying colts to start i got wind of three colts that were in a divorce situation and were for sale stephanie and i went to look at them and they were pretty thin two of them were two year olds and one was a four year old they had been feeding them in one pile so the four year old wasent near as thin as the other but he sure wasent fat either i bought all three for nine hundred dollars including papers i got them home and turned the two year olds out and started the four year old other than bucking me off once he made a nice horse the next spring i started the two year olds one of them is who this story is about badger is what i called this colt he was brown with a strip face and four white socks when i started him he was gentle but i got busy and turned him back out for the summer that fall i caught him up and shod him and started rideing him boy was he different he wouldent buck but my god was he goosey and high strung the first thing that happened is i rode up to a wire gate to open it i got off him and a truck drove by us out on the highway he jumped right thru that wire gate and destroyed it but never got cut at all the next thing is pop and i were rideing down this creek the bank was about ten foot above the water on our side and no bank on the other side there were pools that were deep well anyway pop got mad at his dog and swung his romal at him and badger whirled and jumped off that bank we lit in one of those deep pools and we went clear under then came up and he swam out on the other side the next thing he decided to be hard to get off of and would jump away when you steped off of him i went to see a horse trader friend of mine and he told me take him down to the arena and gallop him ten laps around it and stop and try to step off if he even shifts his weight do ten more laps keep that up until he stands for you to step off i did that all afternoon and he finely gave it up and was never hard to get off again after i rode him about six months one day he just gave up on all those bad habits and got real gentle and really wanted to do good i kept on rideing him and the next fall i went to a big horse show and showed him i didnt place but i did pretty good and im sure i was the onley one there on a three hundred dollar horse

Jim W. Barrie

Mollie and The Eater Egg Hunt

when stephanie and I got married we lived right next to the thermalands
fire station we had a small dog named mollie she was a sheltie fox terrier
cross and loved everyone especially kids at the fire house they had
pancake breakfasts twice a year and mollie always attended with or
without us and came home after everyone left stephanie had nieces and
nephews and when they got old enough for easter egg hunting they
would come and stay with aunt steph and uncle jim for the easter egg
hunt at the fire house mollie loved these visits and went every where
with those kids including the easter egg hunt and helped them find eggs
about the second year she found an egg and ate it and found out they
were good to eat the next year we got up and were getting the kids ready
for the hunt and we let mollie outside pretty soon there was a knock on
the door and one of the firemen had mollie with him it seems she had
gone down and started the easter egg hunt early he told us she was still
invited but to send her down after all the kids got there

Daisey

daisy was raised right down the road from us she was out of woodrows
stud and a sugar bars mare she was with a brown gelding that had an old
wire cut on him my dad bought both of them for chickenfeed as the guy
that owned them said she was 4 and barely halter broke and the brown
gelding was crippled I went over there horseback and caught the brown
horse and led him and daisy followed us to the red barn when we got
them down there we looked the brown horse over and he wasent
crippled pop said that guy said that brown horse was broke if you will try
him out for me and ride him for a month I will give you the mare that
sounded like a deal to me so I tried the brown out he was gentle didn't
know much but fine I got daisy halter broke a little better and started her

122

she was easy to get along with and real quick I had been working for a
man that was one of the best bridal men in central Nevada so daisy was
my project she came right along and made a real nice spade bit horse
every one in the country new her and every little kid in the country rode
her around sometimes three or four at a time she was the kind of horse
that no matter what you had to do or what kind or storm you got in she
always did her part all you had to worry about was your part we did a lot
of jobs and covered a lot of country together probably our finest day was
when we roped a steer of my cousins going wide open down the two way
left turn lane on north beale road I caught the steer and she was smart
enough to stop real easy so she didn't slip the cars pulled over for us and
we drug him out in a vacant lot and tied him down till pop and my cousin
came with the gooseneck ive had many horses since but none I trusted as
much as daisy

Running the Family Ranch

after stephanie and I got married I ran the family ranch and started and
resold quite a few colts I would buy five at a time and start them and sell
three of them and keep the two I liked the best and sell them when I got
them finished its interesting that then I had trouble selling them close to
home now that im older people want to buy horses all the time now that
I don't resell horses anymore this went on for a few years I also shod
horses and dayworked and gathered small bunches of cattle for people
that couldent get them it was kind of a culture shock to work by myself
and what you learn to do to catch some of those spoiled cows but I had
two good dogs and some good horses so I did pretty good also most of
the daywork I had done I was pretty picky about who it was for some of
these jobs were unique one day I was reading the local paper and saw an
ad looking for a trapper in our county so I applied and got the job it was

just for the summer but it opened some doors for me and it was something I could do and do well

Trapping Part Time

after I got the trapping job I worked part time and when they needed me for several years between that I day worked rode horses and shod horses we had a great ag commissener and he kept trying to get me on full time I worked a lot with the federal trapper and he had a lot of time in and was a phenonamal person and trapper I was just starting out and I wanted to catch and shoot everything one day I asked that older trapper what he was going to do when he retired he said im going to put this damed rifle in the closet and let the barrell rust shut at the time I didn't understand that but after several years I understood it the other thing I had to learn about was office politics and backstabbing I always found it interesting that everyone thought working on ranches was so bad but the worst ranches I worked on had your back a lot more than government hire

Little Old Man

when i was growing up every ranch had a little old man on it sometimes these old guys worked there sometimes they just lived there sometimes they owned the place these old guys were always busy doing something never alot but something all the time they knew what was going on around the place that was a great help when i became a trapper some of those old guys were also real good trackers and could sure save you alot of time if you bothered to talk to them i was raised to respect older people and always liked to visit with old timers anyway so i got along with those old guys pretty well one thing i always noticed is as long as that old guy was there things stayed fixed up but you let that guy move to town or pass away and see how fast one of those places falls apart i was talking to my friend joe the other day he had tractor mike at the ranch he manages he told me when mike was around i never had to run my own parts or anything he knew what kind of oil everything uses and kept it in stock and also fixed alot of things and kept the shop organised i sure miss him and almost need to hire someone to run parts around here instead of me running my own parts in my trapping career i saw the last of the little old men on ranches as they all died or moved to town but this place is sure alot poorer place without them

Sensitivity Training

after I had worked trapping for about a year we got called to go to sensitivity training with the federal trappers we went down by napa and camped on this lake they had some buildings for meetings and we were there for three days all of sacramento district and northern district were there and maybe some of central district we covered all kinds of things we needed to know and then came sensitivity training we were all in this building and were watching this film it would have a situation and then they would shut the film off and discuss it then turn the film on and show you how you should have handled it this one particular situation was this bank president was retireing and got drunk at his party and told the guy getting his job the only reason he got that job was he was a kiss ass they turned the film off and said how would you guys handle that some guys said ignore it some guys said just figure he had to much to drink somebody in the back of the room where they couldent see said catch him in the parking lot the next day and kick his ass the lights came back on and did we get a lecture about why we were all there it made the day about two hours longer than it should have been but we sure thought it was funny

The One I Couldn't Catch

when I first started trapping I really liked trapping coyotes with steel traps I was trapping in the federal trappers area of our county one summer while he was in the mountains and I ran across this big male coyote and I couldent catch him to save my life I would spend hours making sets and go back and cheack them and he would walk up to my trap and dig down real easy till he felt metal and take a crap there and walk away he did that to me all summer and fall when john came home from the mountains that fall I told him about that coyote he said he thought he could catch him I asked him years later if he got him he told me he never could catch him but one day he shot him that's the story of the one I never could catch

Lion Under the Trailer

when I was trapping part time one day all the county and federal trappers got called to go to a meeting and I was the only one in the county the ag office got a call about a lion in a subdivision up interstate eighty so I went up there this woman had fed her cat outside and he was eating and a lion jumped out of the brush and killed her cat so I get there and this woman is hysterical because she has small kids I set our lion trap and that night the federal trapper called me and said meet him there at daylight so next morning we meet at the house and it had snowed about six inches so we look around and find lion tracks thru the snow he lets me out and goes to look around the edge of the subdivision im following these tracks and find where he walked right by this mobile home and the tracks turn and look like they went under it I think he surely cant be under that trailer and im looking around for another track some where about then john comes back and I tell him what I found and I cant find any other tracks he takes a flash lite and looks under this trailer sure enough that lion is under there he goes around an opens the crawl space on the other side and I hit the skirting with a stick on my side the lion tears out of there and we turned the hounds loose they treed him in about a hundred yards and we killed him we took it by the house where the cat got killed and the guy that lived there said man im glad you got him my wife went to her mothers last and I wasent going to get a home cooked meal till you killed him

Bear Call in Subdivision

we used to get a lot of bear calls to take care of this one time we got a call about a bear breaking into houses in this subdivision this bear was pretty smart because all the houses were two story and he would climb up the support that held the porch upstairs and go thru the sliding glass door most people just had a screen door up there anyway we took the bear trap up there and set it and he went two houses down and broke in another house we chased him around that neighborhood for about a week before we caught him in the mean time everybody thought he would like there garbage better so they thru a bag of garbage in our trap for bait boy was that trap a mess to clean when we got him

Bear Call at Snowflower

another bear call I got was to go up interstate eighty to a camp ground and look at a camp trailer a bear got in I got up there and this camp trailer was brand new they had just bought it and took it up there it didn't even have licence plates on it yet a bear had got in over the sink and ate everything in there including about thirty pacages of microwave popcorn and then tore the entire back out of the trailer when he left I set the bear trap right next to the trailer and didn't catch him but the next day I found his tracks on a little road in back so I moved my trap out there and caught him that night there were some animal lovers that said I caught an innocent bear and I wondered if I had also altho I was pretty sure I had the right one when we got him out of the trap there was no dought I caught the right one because there was bear crap with micro wave popcorn in it about six inches deep in the bottom of the trap what a mess

Sour Dough Biscuits

1 cup flour
1 ½ cups starter
½ Tablespoon baking powder
½ tablespoon sugar
¼ teaspoon salt
2 tablespoons oil

Mix flour, baking powder, sugar and salt in a bowl. Pour in starter.
Make firm dough. I add oil at this point. Flatten dough out and cut
biscuits. Grease pan. I use a 8 inch cast iron frying pan. Crowd
biscuits in pan and let rise 30 minutes. Bake in 400 degree oven 24 to
30 minutes.

As I wrote this cookbook, I felt I should mention some of the great ranch
women who inspired me and Stephanie and taught us about their ways.

Helen Anne Barrie

Helen Anne Barrie was my mother. She grew up on a sheep ranch
cooking for lambing crews. When weused to ship cows to the mountains
the cows and us arrived at the same time and myself, my dad and my
sister had to go unload trucks and mother up everything. All mom
needed to set up camp were the bedrolls packed in, the groceries
unloaded and a bucket of water packed in. Mom taught me how to cook
and a lot of the camp hints in this book.

Mary Jenson

Mary and her husband Jim lived outside of Wheatland on a irrigated ranch. Im was a big touch sheepshearer, bear hunter and cowman. Mary was what every ones grandmother should be. You just wanted to crawl up in her lap and put your arms around her neck. Mary was a great cook and she truly enjoyed feeding people. She was a great inspiration to Stephanie. Mary thought if you got there too late for breakfast you needed to stay for lunch. If you were too late for lunch, be there for supper. If you missed supper, roll your bed out in the bunkhouse and be there for breakfast the next morning.

Pat and Marie Wilson

Pat and Marie were 2 sisters who married 2 brothers Harold and Carroll Wilson and they all lived in the same house for the better part of 50 years. The Wilson brothers started out with nothing and ended up with a lot of cows and ranches. They used to hire me in the spring for branding and shipping. When we branded no matter where it was at noon, Pat and Marie came driving up in the car and opened the trunk and brought out a home cooked hot huge meal complete with desert. They were also a huge inspiration to Stephanie and a huge part of my life also.

Shipping Lambs

my friend dan tells a story about shipping sheep. it reminded me of when
i was about nine years old we got caught up at haypress camp and had a
real good man hired that summer so we went to help moms aunt ship
lambs moms aunt velma and her pardner jean ran sheep down here they
had several bands then in the summer they went to martis valley and
summered three or four bands around there their camp was at the end of
martis valley on martis creek we got there and unloaded our bedrolls and
had supper it was fantastic jean was a great basque cook and we had a
great supper they had butchered several lambs and would hang them out
at nite and take them down and wrap them in a tarp during the day right
outside the cookhouse they had a board and they would hang a huge
ham on it at nite then in the morning they would get that ham and cut
slices off of it and cook ham and scrambled eggs and hot cakes for
breakfast some times we ate before daylite or some days we just had a
snack in the mourning and then a huge breakfast after the trucks were
loaded after sleeping out on the ground all nite i can still remember those
meals the next day another band would come into the corralls and ship
the herders were all basque and nice to kids everyday in the afternoons
we would go look for arrowheads in the meadow we found a few but we
wernt real good at that after a week down there we went back to camp
and got ready to start gathering but i have never forgoten shipping lambs
and those meals

Listening to Pop off Pops Point

when I ride out on pops point above bear river we always used to gather
that and he always went off that steep point and crossed across to a big
canyon to this day I don't know where he crossed and have to go around
he did tell me once he wouldent try and cross It on any other horse than

Jim W. Barrie

the one he rode at the last when he dropped of the end we would wait
for him a while so we wernt ahead of him when he pushed any cattle out
of there so you could hear him down there working his dogs he had real
good dogs but as he aged he got deaf and pretty loud it was mollie come
back you son of a bitch oh I wish I had you head under my boot right now
I ought to kill you when we get out of here godam it harry I said come
back if I had somebody working for me that had dogs like you id fire him
what in the hell ails you two anyway are you mentaly retarded or what
but when he got out of there he always had all the cattle that were in
there and those dogs worked good for him a lot of people asked him
what his favorite dog was and he always said what ever one I have at the
time

Helping Mac At Soldier Meadow

the other day stephanie spoke about going to soldier meadows so i
thought i would tell you about when i first went out there my job down
here was getting to me pretty bad and one day i came home and
stephanie told me she had a surprise for me she had called my old friend
john and told him i needed to go buckarooing for a while and i was
supposed to call him i called him and he said i will send you down to
soldier meadows to help mac as i cant find anyone that likes being that
far out on the desert i had worked with john at the gambel ranch and for
him at red rock lake so i took a weeks vacation and went out there just
like she told you the road for the first twenty miles was awful but i made
it and drove up to the houses and asked for mac he invited me in and said
whats the deal here john said he was sending a cowboy down here and i
dont need someone i need to babysit and shoe horses for i replied well
ive worked around alot and i can shoe a horse as well as anyone makeing
a liveing at it the bad news is im only here for the next nine days but
short of rideing cranky horses im up for anything he said ok unload your

stuff in the barn and roll your bed out in that little bunk house across from the cook house that evening at supper he told me we would move a bunch of pairs to summit lake the next day and we were going early because it was so hot the next morning we ate breakfast at three oclock and saddled up and troted over to a place called antelope springs it was just the two of us and the irragator so we bunched about six hundred pair up and headed for summit lake these were all cross bred brahma cows and the calfs had some size so they really strung out and went it was one of the neatist things i saw all those cows strung out one behind each other going up the road just as the sun was comeing up we got them up to sumit lake by noon and then rode back and had a sandwich and went out and shod two horses i did one and mac did the other the rest of the week was move cows some where everyday and shoe a couple horses after lunch mac was a great one to plan his work and i really learned alot from him that i still use today i used to like hearing macs stories and then hear the same story from candy it was interesting to hear there seperate thoughts on the same thing that was the third time mac had worked at soldier meadows and we knew alot of the same guys all to soon my vacation was up but i promised mac and candy i would come back and bring my wife next time

Pops Point

I always go out on pops point when I ride its a high windy point above bear river I always air my horses back and reset my saddle and just look around you can see so much and so many memories I started going with pop and grandpa when I was 5 up here ill soon be 63 that's 57 years on one side or the other of the river many thoughts go thru my head every where I look from here I remember someone who has moved away or passed away or is still around look across the river I spent a lot of time over there with loren and his crew I remember when we trailed all those wild cows of miguils out of there I can see the river from where im at it looks full the last time pop and I crossed it he was 85 it was really high to be crossing and swift but we made it got 8 pairs of ours from buck and his crew they helped us get them in the water and stayed there till we came out on the other side everybody waved and said see you next year six weeks later pop was dead look up the river I can see big hill I spent a lot of time with Harold and carroll and danny up there we rode a lot of miles gathering up there I can also see government hill where john and jody and I hunted and trapped also ran hounds some I think back on all the faces names different horses and dogs that country has seen I remember when the river was high and the woodcutters built a bridge across it was made of digger pine logs and notched to gether except for the deck there wasent a nail in it lorens kids were little then now there grown and have kids of there own I look across and up and see matts old place I used to daywork for him now hes moved away as I sit there and reflect I think dam 57 years went by quick I guess theres a lesson in this for the young people

Shes hauled water from the creek. Dust all over her clothes. She's been so hot she thought she would die and so cold she nearly froze. Whether things are good or bad, right by him she will stand. She's the wife behind the cowboy and the cowboys a lucky man.

Jim and Stephanie Driving Miss Daisy

Lincoln 4th of July Parade

Made in the USA
Las Vegas, NV
01 May 2023

71422828R00083